Another
HILL and
Sometimes
a MOUNTAIN

Tim Green

ISBN: 9781724109415

First printing October 2018

Editing by Marlayna Glynn

Interior Formatting, Layout & Design by David Scott

Dedication
To Ray

CONTENTS

FOREWORD

L et me introduce you to my friend, Tim Green.
Tim is a very handsome man. He has blond hair and eyes the color of sea glass. He's well-groomed and in perfect shape. His smile dazzles. If you were to meet him, you would think, *Now there goes a guy who's really got it together. Life has clearly been good to him.*

Which is why you need to read this book.

Because Tim Green has overcome obstacles in his life that most of us can only imagine. The fact that he has achieved all that he has — the fact that he is actually still here with us at all — is remarkable. It's a testament to the optimism and courage that he brings to every adventure and every day.

Which isn't to say that there haven't been plenty of times that I've wanted to deck him. Like when I'm about to collapse in a workout, and he starts singing "The Sun Will Come Out Tomorrow." Or that time he talked me into a charity dance-a-thon and then insisted that we wear matching flapper girl outfits. Or all the times I've said "no presents" and he's shown up dressed as Santa Claus with a bag of goodies on his back. But what's the point of getting exasperated? That's just Tim being Tim: a guy who believes that there is no one — and no situation — that won't be improved by a smile, a hug, and just the right amount of flair.

Tim is the Pied Piper of children. All children; no exceptions, ever. When my boys were little, their friends used to say to them, "Hey, can that big kid come over and play, too?" Doesn't matter whether the child is 3 months or 15 years old — they're all helpless in the force field of his personality. One day a long time ago, I watched him walk into a ward full of severely developmentally disabled kids. He never hesitated. He went from one to the other, talking, smiling, taking their hands in his as if there was nothing different about them at all. And one by one I watched their usually blank faces light up, their heads turn, and their hearts responding to what in many cases their eyes couldn't see. When you read his story, you'll see that no one could have blamed him if he had decided he was done with kids once he was an adult. But that's not who he chooses to be. As my husband John says, Tim treats everyone the way he would like to be treated, no matter how many times he gets knocked down in the process.

Now John also wants you to understand that he knew Tim before I did, okay? He met him at an aerobics class. Which he walked out of because Tim started high-kicking to a Whitney Houston song. Tim dragged him back in. I don't think he ever got John high-kicking — or appreciating Whitney Houston — but he sure got him as a friend.

And when we lost our first child, and I couldn't get up off the floor, Tim just showed up and sat by my side. And somehow he got me to stand, and then to walk. And then he stayed with us the whole way down into that valley, back up the mountain, and safely to the other side. Thirty years later, he's still here — a third parent to our boys and a family member in all but birth. What we've learned about him along the way is that behind the dazzling smile and crazy energy is a heart made deep and strong by the road he's had to walk. *Another Hill and Sometimes a Mountain* is the story of that journey.

I'm glad he's finally sharing it with all of you.

Bess Armstrong
Los Angeles

Acknowledgments

Many blessings to Creator, and many blessings to
Mother Earth. Thank you for connecting me to the
highest light, the highest love, the highest of sounds
and vibrations on all levels of existence.

To Mayadah and Anne Marie for your spiritual
cleansing and guidance.

To Liese for your belief and talent.

To my family and friends who have been with me on
this journey from the beginning.

To Marlayna for helping me shepherd my words out
into the world. You are simply the best.

PROLOGUE

Another hill and sometimes the mountain
Another road with rocks to hurt my feet
But He walks along beside me
I can make it, there will be no retreat.

— George D. McGraw

When I was very young, and living in the midst of chaos and uncertainty, I learned this country ballad at church. The simple words gave my little worried mind a great sense of hope; the gentle chords soothed my heart. The words to this song have rung true my entire life, as my road had a lot of rocks to hurt my feet. Yet when I think of the many people who have been a part of my journey and feel a great sense of gratitude for their participation. In writing this book, I continue to not only look for personal healing but to help others on their journeys. Each of our individual stories have meaning and are worth telling; we have a choice in how we accept our circumstances and use those experiences.

It could be said that my childhood was negative, dark, and lonely. That's certainly one way to look at it. While it's true that many of my childhood waking moments were peppered with my desire to stay safe, I held on to the belief that something better was going to happen; something fantastic was going to come my way. Even though I lived a fear-based life and was required to abide by established rules, I created a safe place in my mind through physical activity. I have now come to realize how amazing those experiences were, and how they've made me the person I am today. This is my story.

Another Hill and Sometimes a Mountain

CHAPTER 1

I was born Timothy Paul Green on November 25, 1959, in a small hospital in Medina, Ohio. Chartered in 1952, the town was indeed small with just over 5,000 residents at the time of my birth. Now with a population of only over 25,000, Medina is ranked #40 on the list of "America's Best Small Towns." Although the recent announcement by Money Magazine naming Medina as one of the top 100 best places to live may have been no surprise for the current residents, it was to me.

I was a blue baby, having been born with what's called a nuchal cord. The umbilical cord — my sole source of oxygen — was wrapped tightly about my neck. Of course, anything that hinders the flow of blood through the umbilical cord can cause a baby to experience birth asphyxia. We receive nutrients and oxygen via the umbilical cord, not by breathing through our nose or mouth. Babies don't actually breathe until after the birth when they take in that first breath of oxygen into their lungs, which happens about two minutes after birth. Despite being born in a small hospital in a small town, you could say I was born just in time. The doctors were able to provide oxygen quickly enough to save my life.

Strike one against my birth mother, Lenore.

After being under observation for several days in the hospital, my mother and I were reunited with my older brother and sister. The single room in the apartment complex where the four of us lived was cramped and crowded, ventilated by only one small window. The neighbors' music blasted all day long, while the stench of beer bottles and trash from down the stairs filtered helplessly up into our room. Dirty clothes lined the stairway leading up to our apartment. My young mother's less-than-stellar housekeeping skills didn't help our situation. Unwashed dishes filled the sink, seeming to attract every fly in the town. As for me, I understand that I spent most of my first year shirtless, clad only in what was usually a dirty diaper.

My birth parents, Lenore and Paul, hailed from Wheeling, West Virginia, a small town located at the foothills of the Appalachian Mountains. Wheeling, like my mother, had a proud beginning. When the Civil War began, Wheeling seceded from Virginia — serving as the provisional capital of the Restored Government of Virginia from 1861 to 1863. An early nickname of the town was "Nail City," due to the iron manufacture in several mills which dated from the 1840s. As Wheeling aged, slums increased, resulting in among other things the necessity to regulate personal cesspools. The town instituted a ban on pipe communications with other homes and businesses "unless offensive smells were properly trapped." Although Wheeling reached its peak of population in 1930, the Great Depression — with changes and restructuring in heavy industry following World War II — led to a loss of working-class jobs and people.

It was into this environment that my birth mother Lenore was born into a large family with ten children: four boys and six girls. Her future husband, Paul, a twin, had six siblings in his family of five boys and two girls. When Lenore was twelve years old, she got pregnant by one of her older brothers. Once Lenore's mother discovered the irrefutable evidence that her daughter was with child, she convinced the man she was sleeping with to marry her daughter to make the pregnancy "right." That man was my birth father, Paul. He was a full decade older than Lenore, just twenty-two years old himself. He agreed to marry my mother but continued his affair with my grandmother. Despite this untraditional arrangement, Lenore and Paul went on to have children of their own.

My brother, Jimmy, was born in 1947. Paul tolerated Jimmy because it was clear from the beginning that Jimmy was different. Paul, who knew of course that Jimmy was not his natural son, had very little interaction with the child and was an absent father from the get-go. Surprisingly, Lenore permitted her brother — Jimmy's father and uncle — to visit the child on a regular basis. The teenaged Lenore went on to carry two more pregnancies to full term, yet both infants were born dead. My sister was born in November of 1957. By the time the couple's first surviving child was born, the stress had become too much for Paul. He departed for greener pastures, leaving Lenore alone with a developmentally disabled son and an infant daughter. One year after my sister's birth, however, Paul made a surprise visit, and I was accidentally conceived.

After a series of explosive encounters between Paul and Lenore, he made the decision to abandon the family for good. Lenore — who couldn't have been more than 22 at the time — likely felt desperate and alone with three young children and no hope for a future. She took a bottle of sleeping pills to end her life. Like most of her endeavors, she failed at that, too. My older brother Jimmy was unable to wake Lenore, but despite his disabilities, thankfully he knew enough to dial the police. It is unknown how much time passed between Lenore falling unconscious before Jimmy picked up the phone though. Upon their arrival, the police and paramedics discovered the sleeping young mother in an apartment that should have been condemned. Among the empty pill and liquor bottles, soiled diapers, and stacks of moldy newspapers, the police discovered three severely neglected children.

Although I was a year old, I was still captive in my tiny prison cell of a crib. The police report described my condition as "severely malnourished," describing my sharp, protruding ribcage, gaunt face, and pasty grey skin color. My hygiene had not been attended to, and evidence of such was also noted in the police report, as it was clear that my diaper had not been changed in the recent past. The smell permeated the one-room apartment, causing the policemen and paramedics to cover their faces in disgust. Most neglected babies in conditions as dire as how the authorities found me do not survive. "Failure to thrive" is the usual cause of death listed for such unfortunate children. However, I had a guardian angel in my sister. Although she was only 18 months older than me, she had been slipping saltine crackers through the bars of my crib. If not for my kind sister's loving acts, I would be dead. The police notified the welfare department of child services and my siblings and I were removed from the home. My sister and I were taken to a foster home. Jimmy was taken to a Children's Home, due to his apparent mental health issues. Lenore was taken to the hospital.

Our first foster parent was Mrs. Smith, who was in her late 50s or early 60s. She was always very well dressed and prided herself on her appearance. Her house, likewise, was immaculate. My three-year-old sister and I were her first foster children, and while she did provide us with a place to live and daily meals, she was quite militant and very strict. She reprimanded us continually. For children who were not taught how to behave by Lenore, my sister and I found this new environment nothing short of baffling. When my sister and I first arrived at Mrs. Smith's home, we knew no boundaries, lacking any sort of instruction on how to behave, eat, sleep, talk, or function. We did not know right from wrong. We did not know what was permissible and what wasn't. When I ran afoul of Mrs. Smith's many standards, she had me lay my hands out in front toward her. She then proceeded to hit them repeatedly with a butter knife. For a one-year-old child who didn't yet understand the world and its plethora of rules, these experiences were altogether physically, mentally, and emotionally traumatic.

At first, child services permitted Lenore and Paul to visit Mrs. Smith's home, and my sister and I were instructed to meet with them outside. The visits were to last anywhere from an hour to an hour and a half — but not a moment longer. Most times we were taken to a nearby park or an ice cream stand. Our parents usually did not visit together, so my sister and I were never privy to their interactions. I do recall that whenever I was given a gift, which was usually a small bag of candy or a used stuffed animal, it was immediately taken away and discarded by Mrs. Smith as soon as I re-entered her home.

Mrs. Smith and Lenore were not fond of each other and usually bickered at each visit. The tension created between the two was mostly due to Mrs. Smith's disapproval of the visits, as well as Lenore's constant ranting that stemmed from her jealousy. Lenore knew she couldn't be the mother Mrs. Smith appeared to be. I recall how the arguments would escalate in pitch, and most times were not rectified by a satisfying conclusion. Later in life, I would come to gain a greater understanding of the depth of those arguments. They always stemmed from the constant grasp for control of how my sister and I were to be treated, handled, and raised. Eventually, the stress of the continuous disagreements became too much for Mrs. Smith, and she decided it would be best to stop fostering my sister and me.

While I was relieved to get out from under the turmoil at Mrs. Smith's house, I was terrified by the questions that loomed large in my mind. Although I was not yet three years old at this time, I was old enough to be more than aware that my environment was about to shift dramatically. I no longer remember whether Mrs. Smith told us we would be leaving, or I overheard conversations between adults, but I became paralyzed by a pervasive, all-encompassing fear. What was going to happen to me? Where was I going? Who would take care of me? Would my sister remain with me? The not knowing was so painful; it hurt on every level.

By the mid-1950s, the U.S. experienced a sharp increase in child population due to a decline in infant mortality rates and the post-WWII baby boom. For example, in 1956 there were 57 million children in the U.S. This increased number of children naturally increased the number of children needing foster care as well. The stretching ratio of children to adults created new challenges in meeting the increasing demands for social workers. Between 1961 and 1967, there was a 50-percent increase in the number of children receiving child welfare services in an average month. Studies also noted that during this time when I was in foster care, the composition of children in foster care changed. Rather than enter care because of family poverty, a more significant percentage of children entering care were for abuse and neglect, parental instability, and substance abuse.

The prevailing philosophy in foster care at the time of my childhood was one of "keep moving." It was the custom for many social workers to regularly move children from one foster home to another to prevent the foster children and foster parents from forming any sort of attachment. This practice kept the families from bonding, which was thought to be detrimental at the time. For children like me, this meant we could be looking at a future of moving every year to year and a half to a new home, with new parents, and new siblings in a new environment.

Therefore, when Mrs. Jones arrived, my sister and I did not know what to expect, and we had no idea what would happen to us. As the first of many assigned social workers, we were unbelievably fortunate that Mrs. Jones was given our case. A gentle, kind, and heart-centered woman, she became a grandmother figure to us. I remember looking into her warm eyes and thinking for the first time that I was going to be okay. As I mentioned, at that time foster children did not stay in one place for very long. It was because of Mrs. Jones' love for her work, and the diligence she took in placing us in a proper home with the Kidds, that we were never moved again. I didn't know until later how lucky we were not to be moved to avoid "bonding." I will always be grateful to Mrs. Jones for her hand in my early years.

CHAPTER 2

I wasn't quite three years old when Mrs. Jones took my sister and me to 1480 Wall Road, where we became two of the twelve children lucky enough to be fostered by Martha and Frank Kidd. The Kidds lived in a run-down four-bedroom farmhouse just outside the city limits of Wadsworth, Ohio — the infamous home of the Blue Tip match. Although Wadsworth was only about a thirty-minute drive from Medina, my new home could just as easily have been on the other side of the galaxy. At first glance, the outside of the property had no curb appeal whatsoever. The driveway and yards were littered with piles of bike parts and oil cans and animal feces. Broken down cars were parked willy-nilly about the property. The farmhouse was clearly in dire need of significant renovation, including at the very least a fresh coat of paint. The inside of the house was no prettier. The appliances were outdated and most needed repair. All of the floors squeaked when you walked on them. No matter how many times they were replaced, the curtains were always torn. The well-worn furniture usually needed at the very least to be repaired, but preferably replaced. The decor was very simple and basic, as everything necessary to furnish the house arrived via the second-hand store. But, for what the home lacked in beauty and style, it more than made up for with love and acceptance.

Frank Kidd was the second born in a West Virginian family with five children. He went as far as the third grade when an unquestioned expectation forced him to leave school to start his work career. At that very early age, Frank became a coal miner until he was drafted into the army. He fought in World War II, where he served for four years. When he returned from the war, he met Martha, and they were soon married by the local Justice of the Peace. They began their life together and had two biological daughters who both lived in the house while I grew up there. Martha was also born in West Virginia, the ninth of seventeen children. Although she was only educated as far as the second grade, she possessed a good amount of common sense, likely acquired by taking care of her eight younger siblings. In her family, the females had been primarily responsible for the parenting, a pattern established by her oldest sister eight siblings above her. Martha, it seemed, was a born natural at child-rearing.

Frank worked long hours as a bricklayer, so Martha was our primary caregiver. Her selfless qualities defined and dominated our household, and she became an instant mother to me. Martha was a simple woman who never wore makeup or styled her hair. She was very timid when she spoke to strangers, as she was embarrassed by the limits of her second-grade education. Although Martha was a small woman, she was powerful and rose to any challenge necessitated by caring for abandoned children. She set a beautiful example of welcoming, love, and kindness, which made it very easy for her kids to learn how to accept anyone and everyone despite their condition or appearance.

Martha rejected no one, and so our door was always open. Our home was a safe haven for kids of all ages, races, and disabilities. My brothers and sisters included those who were blind, burn victims, amputees, in wheelchairs, mentally challenged, hearing impaired, pregnant, and in later years, drug babies. We were all taught to be strong, to treat each other with respect, and above all — to be grateful.

Martha was very matter-of-fact in her instruction, which shaped us in many ways. She taught us about every disability, and how the disabled were not much different from us. We just needed to take special care with these individuals. For example, when a new kid arrived with a disability, Martha would good-naturedly introduce them to us and say, for example, "This is Shirley. Sometimes when you are playing a game away from home, Shirley might fall down and start to move uncontrollably. When this happens, do not be afraid. Stay calm and act swiftly. Move everything away from her and let her finish what is called a seizure. When she stops moving, she will be exhausted. Pick her up, bring her home, and put her to bed." That was the no-nonsense way we learned about how to help someone who was having a seizure. Tommy, who was deaf, needed to be in front of you when you spoke to him so he could read your lips. Sarah arrived in her wheelchair, and so we had to learn how to transfer and lift her properly.

We were raised in the school of common sense. In the winter months, Martha would tell us to wear a coat when it was cold outside. If we chose not to listen to her instruction and fell sick, then it would be our own fault. We learned to make our own decisions, and we were held responsible for the consequences. For example, we were never punished for our grades in school. As long as we did well, and didn't get into trouble, we were not bothered about how we were doing. We weren't questioned or monitored about homework, school projects, or anything regarding our progress. I'm not entirely sure how the lot of us made it through our education. We had no one to tutor or help us, yet somehow we made it work. I believe this was mostly because neither Frank nor Martha had enough education to help us much. With that being said, I genuinely think they did the best they could do with what they had to work with.

Frank, a strong man of few words, stood 6'2" and was very handsome and quite rugged. Like Martha, he had a taciturn demeanor. I used to love to stand by the sink to watch him shave in the mornings. My job was to point out if he missed a spot. I recall that his hair was always perfect, and I liked the way he combed his hair. I comb my hair to this day in the exact same way. That was our most familial connection. Frank worked 12–14 hours a day for the company that owned the house he and Martha rented for $200 a month. Yet when he arrived home, he became the disciplinarian, a chore Martha seemed more than happy to delegate to him. I loved doing silly things to make this stern man laugh. For example, I loved to make noises. When people visited our house, I would make a noise associated with one of their movements. Frank would laugh at their startled reaction or the fact that they tried to ignore my sound effects. For him, it was a real treat to watch our visitors wonder what those crazy noises were.

At some point during his service in World War II, Frank's thumb was shot off, and the absence of this digit was endlessly fascinating to me. When he was in a good mood, Frank would sometimes tell us fantastic stories about how he'd lost his thumb. Each story was different down to the details but always held my undivided attention whether it was because of a bomb, gunshot, or a machete. Each story was a treasure trove of excitement for my little ears to feast upon. No matter the telling, the tale invariably ended with him having his thumb in his pocket. He never showed it to us, but we always believed he carried it with him.

In Ohio, biological parents must sign release forms for their child to be adopted. Lenore could have signed the release at any time, but she stubbornly refused to relinquish her rights for reasons she would take to her grave. Because Paul had walked out on Lenore, he lost the privilege of participating in my fate. This made Lenore the sole decision maker, yet she refused to make a decision. The Kidds would not legally adopt me anyway because they did not want to lose the financial benefits they received for my care, a mere $1.89 per day. With twelve children under their roof, the Kidds were dependent upon the income. So it was that from the age of twelve months to eighteen years, I remained in the foster care system. During this time, I went through 44 social workers and encountered over 189 fellow foster children.

CHAPTER 3

To me, our home was magical, as the property was populated with many farm animals including chickens, cows, pigs, horses, and dogs. One of my favorite places on the property was the barn, a massive two-story building that was much bigger than our house where hay was kept from the fields around our house. The barn had little rooms that I could decorate, and where I could entertain all the animals. It was there where I met my first pet, Arnold, the pig.

Along with the other children, I made forts and pretended to be in "the city." Although the Kidds were never unkind to us, they were not our birth parents, and so we loved to create places in the hay to help us forget and escape from where we were for just a little while. I spent many hours building forts with my brothers and sisters. In the summers, we would have sleepovers in the barn loft. I also enjoyed the mile-and-a-half-long driveway that led from Wall Road to the farmhouse. On that driveway, I ran away my troubling emotions, found fossils, and shoveled snow every winter. The property also boasted a stunning apple, plum, cherry, and pear tree orchard which became my private sanctuary when I could sneak away. I loved the orchard, as most of my dreams were created there. It was

eat place to escape from a hectic household with
.ildren. I climbed the highest cherry tree and ate to
.. .rt's content until my lips and fingers and shirt were
stained cherry red. I dreamt of the many possibilities my
life might bring.

I absolutely loved having so many brothers and sisters.
During the eighteen years I lived with the Kidds, I was able
to experience and transition from being the youngest to
the oldest child in the family. New arrivals to the Kidd clan
were to us like getting a new toy. Whenever a new boy
arrived, all the other boys jumped in and showed him
where to sleep and explained how to do the chores. When
the new arrival was a female, the girls did the same for her.
It was a markedly different environment from Mrs. Smith's
home, as the Kidd household was much more relaxed with
lots of positive energy and excitement. The only downside
was having to say goodbye to a brother or sister, which
caused such a conflict of emotions inside me. I always felt
happy for a child when their parents came back to get
them, or they were adopted into a new home. But I was still
sad to see them go, as each child became an essential part
of our family. I knew that I would probably never see them
again, so it didn't take long for me to understand what it
meant to be a foster child. Most of the children who came
to the home were just held until their parents could take
them back. In the case of my sister and me, Lenore and Paul
never came back for us.

I loved and trusted Martha Kidd very much; however, I
found myself continually working to win her approval. I
watched her carefully, memorizing her every move so I
could anticipate anything she needed before she even knew
she needed it. I made sure all of her belongings were

organized. I made her coffee in the morning. I cleaned and polished her shoes, and ironed her dresses. This was one of the many ways I created security to make sure that I would not be moved, making myself "indispensable." Eventually, by doing so, I became Martha's favorite. She trusted me, giving me responsibilities that none of the other kids were awarded.

As foster children of the Kidds, we were provided with new clothing three times a year, at Christmas, Easter, and for the beginning of each school year. This purchase would invariably include two pairs of pants, two shirts, a jacket or sweater, a package of underwear, T-shirts, three pairs of socks, and a single pair of shoes. I was always voted to go and pick out everyone's clothes because it became clear that I had style and impeccable taste. I loved going shopping, and eagerly anticipated the reactions to the new clothing. My homecoming was always full of joy and satisfaction; just one of the many ways I elicited the secret approval I so desperately needed.

I was a very small child, and so my clothes always needed to be altered. Sewing was yet another way I learned to find joy. I loved the process of altering my clothing because I could make them the way I wanted them to be. I learned to sew at a very young age while watching my sisters do the "inside chores." It was apparent that I had a natural flair for using patterns and enhancing the clothing I would get from the store. For example, I would open the outside seams of my pants, cut up old flannel shirts and attach them into the open seams, making the most fabulous bell bottoms. As they were a very exclusive trend in the early seventies, I also made vests, shirts, and dresses. I would save the extra fabrics so that I could make quilts.

I've made well over 50 quilts and have gifted every one of them.

With so many kids to manage, punishment was very much a part of my growing up, which wasn't all that unusual for the 1960s and 70s. Even in doling out punishment, the Kidds were fair: we always knew what the discipline was going to be and exactly why we would be receiving it. The penalty could include a slap or being whipped by a switch or a belt. If we did something particularly unacceptable that warranted Martha's "now you are really going to get it!" wrath, we were instructed to go to the giant old weeping willow tree in the backyard and pick a switch. When we brought it back, we would be whipped with it. I remember thinking I was smarter than Martha because I was determined to find a switch that would break easily during my whipping. I soon learned that weeping willow branches don't break. They sting ... a lot!

The next level of punishment usually resulted from Martha's overwhelming frustration and intolerance around the boys' behavior. If there was a fight in the house and I was anywhere near it — regardless of how I tried to avoid it — I would be considered guilty just because I was a boy. Martha would wait until Frank got home from work to inform him of our reckless behavior. Next, he would give us the belt. As part of his whipping technique, he would hold me by one arm and whip me. I figured out that if I ran in a circle fast enough, he would get dizzy and stop the beating. There were positive things that came from being often punished. We sure learned the rules, and we knew we were expected to abide by them.

My obsessive goal to avoid being moved and to remain safe in the Kidd's home was a constant event during that time. Each time I was punished in some form, I reached my arms out, with tears streaming down my face and lips aquiver. With deep heart pangs of sorrow, I would ask Martha to hug me. Receiving this hug was paramount because it assured me that I wouldn't be sent away. I think she knew that if she didn't hug me, it would be a far worse punishment than the whipping itself.

Over the years, I witnessed the continual ushering of kids out of the house due to their unacceptable behavior. The lack of any verbal assurance that I was going to remain in the home kept me in an ambiguous state until I was eighteen years old. I was acutely aware of my surroundings and tried to avoid anything that could cause trouble or threaten my stability. I knew it was vital that I formulate a strategy around how to get what I wanted, which was to stay in Martha and Frank's home. I did not want to be moved to another foster home and became painfully cognizant of the fact that it could happen to me at any time. I witnessed what it took to prompt a move by observing the many brothers and sisters who came through the house. Any act of delinquency such as skipping school, fighting, or refusing to follow the simple orders of the house could prompt change. Invariably, it would not be long before Child Services was called and a social worker would arrive to transport the child to another home. I observed this pattern for several years until my simple yet effective strategy became clear: I could choose to be happy, or I could choose to be sad. If I showed any sign of anger, which I sometimes witnessed in the other children, I knew it would increase my chances of being moved. I realized that if I wanted to stay with the Kidds — and I surely did — then I would need a survival strategy to help me not to feel so angry.

Anger was deeply ingrained in me, and I was aware of its aching presence at all times. This was when I learned about fear, for I was absolutely terrified that if I let that anger flow, it would ultimately take over me and I wouldn't be able to stem the tide. I watched many of my fellow foster kids arrive in our home, only to let their anger get the best of them. They didn't have the tools to deal with the complicated, intense feelings that are so common to foster children. Most kids chose particular ways to express their feelings. Some fought. Some bullied others. Some pulled the hair from their heads. Others chose behaviors such as constant rocking motions or screaming at the top of their lungs. Most of these kids were repeatedly moved until they aged out of the system and by then, many of them found drugs to use as an escape, got pregnant, went on welfare, or robbed stores. Eventually, all of them did jail or prison time.

I understood that because like them I had many reasons to be angry. I felt abandoned. Neglected. Unloved. Many of my questions went unanswered. I wanted to act out, cry, scream, or just hit something to get that incessant flow of anger out of my body. But I knew the risk was way too high. I wasn't willing to give in to the intensity of the anger. I refused to be pushed to the point where I would snap. Sometimes I felt fearful that I might hurt someone. I would then turn the anger on myself and bite my hand until the anger inside of me dissipated. On my hand, between my thumb and forefinger, I had a callus as thick as the soles of my shoes. This behavior continued through my childhood and into my teen years.

No one noticed or really even cared about me, or what I was doing, so I was on my own in making decisions that were directly related to staying safe. When I was five years old, I discovered that whenever I felt that strong emotion building within me, if I ran to the end of the long driveway and back then almost magically, I would no longer be angry. Running then became my anger outlet. Year after year after year I ran, and boy did I have many reasons to run. As I got older, my body recognized this condition and my attitude would instantly change. I ran anywhere from eight to fifteen miles a day. As my anger dissipated, I would feel flooded with joy and find myself singing as my feet hit the driveway. I loved to sing, mostly the joyous songs I learned in church. My exposure to music was limited to country or church music, so "Oh Happy Day" or "The Sun Will Come Out Tomorrow" were two of my go-to songs. As long as I was running, I knew I would be okay. Running was my secret outlet, and I did not want to share it with anyone, for fear that someone could take it away from me.

As a child, it was not uncommon for me to withhold information from the adult world so that I could remain safe. By the first grade, I was already on high alert — protective of my constructed world with the hope to never get into trouble with the Kidds. But I couldn't sustain the complicated construction. My quiet place was always in the highest tree in the orchard, but I couldn't stay there 100% of the time, so in spite of my hyper-intensive efforts, I naturally found myself having to navigate various mishaps.

During recess at school in first grade, while playing airplanes at the top of the slide, I lost my footing and fell twelve feet from the top, landing smack on my head on the blacktop below. Some time passed before a couple of student teachers found me lying prostrate on the ground. Inexplicably, I was not taken to the hospital but instead seated at my desk where I lay unconscious until the end of the school day. When the bell rang, I was put on the bus where I made my way to the very last seat and fell asleep again. It was not until the final inspection round in the bus garage that evening that I was discovered, taken home, and deposited at the end of my driveway. Buried in shame and fear because I was late getting home and terrified of getting in trouble, I quietly made my way up the driveway, snuck in through the back door, and went straight to my bed, and I cried myself to sleep. I was never examined but later learned that it was apparently a concussion. I kept my injury a secret in fear that it could result in me being sent to another home.

The next incident happened that winter while ice skating with the neighboring children. We were playing a game called crack-the-whip on the nearby pond. This is a game where you hold each other's hand and follow the leader in whatever pattern and speed he or she chooses. Since I was the smallest, I was always happy to be the last one on the "whip." This one time as we spun in a circle, the child in front of me fell, and his ice skate blade cut five to six inches deep into my leg. It didn't hurt going in as much as it did coming out, and I was fortunate not to have bled to death. I was so terrified that I would get in trouble that I didn't tell anyone about the wound for three days, even though I could barely walk. The pain was so overwhelming and unparalleled by anything my little body had experienced to that point.

Finally, despite the potential consequences, I knew I had to speak up and was immediately taken to the doctor where I was the beneficiary of 88 stitches in my thigh. The physician said that I could have developed gangrene in the wound and that I was lucky to have dodged amputation. Once again, I was in that familiar place of not feeling safe enough to speak up, complain, or display any negative emotions. In fear of being relocated, I was continually trying to figure out how to become the perfect boy. I was willing to go through immense pain on all levels to keep myself safe. Not surprisingly, this would be a pattern I carried with me well into my adulthood.

CHAPTER 4

Despite the home's shortcomings, somehow we were able to accommodate twelve kids and two adults in a four-bedroom house with one bathroom and a 30-gallon water tank. When it came time to bathe, the oldest sibling was the first to wash, and then he or she would exit without draining the tub. The next oldest would then bathe and likewise, save the water. This pattern would continue all the way down to the very youngest. When I was the youngest, by the time, it was my turn the water was surprisingly still warm but black as night. In addition to having the cleanest bath water, the oldest child also had their own bedroom while everybody else had a single mattress to sleep on upstairs.

We spent most of our days playing outside, and like most kids who grew up in the '60s and '70s, we only came inside at dinner time. There were two long picnic tables on the porch where we ate during the warm summer months. However, when the temperatures dropped, we had to find different places in the house to eat, which mostly resulted in sitting on the floor. Martha bought everything in bulk, so we always ate our meals buffet style. Our daily staple was pinto beans with cornbread, likely because it was an affordable way to feed such a big family. In the summer we had a garden, and Martha canned the vegetables so we could have them in the winter. We watched very little television, but when we did it was usually *The Wizard of Oz* and other movies that are now deemed classics. We had a black & white television for the longest time, and when we finally got a colored one, it was the best surprise ever. I didn't know any different and accepted the circumstances as they were presented to me. Growing up in the Kidds' home never seemed to be a struggle because it was all I knew. Only years later would I realize that I had purposely constructed a very happy life for myself.

All of the chores were delegated, and the whole house was run like a well-oiled machine. Everyone on the Kidd farm had duties. The kids who had been there before me taught me my responsibilities, as I later did with others. The girls usually did the cleaning within the house, while the boys were responsible for all of the outdoor chores. Within the family, I was unique in the fact that I performed tasks inside and outside the home, becoming very efficient at them all. I was primarily in charge of washing, drying, and ironing the clothes and the bedding, as well as folding and putting away the towels and clothes for each kid. Inside I also swept, mopped and waxed the floors, as well as cleaned the windows. The chore I did not care much for was shoveling the coal into the basement.

During the summers, I tended to the garden by weeding, hoeing, and mowing the grass, while in the winter months I shoveled snow from the mile-and-a-half-long driveway. At a very early age, I developed the need to please, partly out of a sense of survival, and because of that, I felt very motivated to learn all that I could. So every day as the sun rose before school, I fed the cows, chickens, and horses, and slopped the pigs. I easily connected with those other living beings in a way that made me feel important. Those beautiful creatures depended on me and showed me the very same unconditional love I had for them. Engaging with the animals positively reinforced my kind and loving nature, and was beneficial for my burgeoning self-esteem.

However, after my beautiful morning with the animals, I headed to school where I underwent a complex array of emotions. While I loved school, I dreaded the social aspect or lack thereof. As I was a small kid clothed in hand-me-downs that were usually at least three times too big (until I learned to sew), I was always teased for my looks as well as my high-pitched voice. I was athletic since I was a runner, so I knew I could easily outrun anyone who chased me and was small enough to hide in a locker which saved me more than a few times.

After school I was either engaged in work or a sport, then I walked home five miles each night to return to the farm for my next set of chores. After my homework was finished, I did the laundry for all fourteen people. This task was not so much forced on me as it represented something I wanted to do to contribute to the household. Like my relationship with the animals, doing the laundry represented a level of responsibility that no one else had. Laundry in the 1960s was nowhere near as convenient or straightforward as it is today. On the farm, we had a wringer washer, which was delicate, old, and would dismantle quite easily. I experienced heightened anxiety knowing I could break the machine and it would affect the massive amounts of laundry that had to be done on a daily basis. Naturally, this was something I desperately tried to avoid. Sometimes I accidentally put more detergent in that old washer than was needed and the suds would overflow on to the basement floor. On these occasions, I ran to get my brothers and sisters so we could fling the suds on our bodies, fashioning beards and funny wigs with the bubbles. We did not have an electric dryer, so the drying process was me hanging the laundry to dry from a long rope strung between two trees. I always tried to color-coordinate the clothes on the line so it would be pleasing to the eye. It was especially challenging during the winter months when the weather prevented outdoor drying; then I was forced to be creative in hanging the clothes from window sills and door frames and furniture.

We had a coal furnace to heat the house. Twice a year, truckloads of coal were delivered, which then needed to be shoveled into the basement. During the colder months, every morning before spending time with the animals or heading off to school, I went to the basement and using newspaper, wood, and coal, I fixed a fire in the furnace. The basement was often flooded, and there was no way to drain the water, which made getting motivated to go into the cellar a tough ask. Once I got the fire going in the furnace, there was no way to regulate the heat. When it got too hot, we had to open the windows.

I was responsible for the mowing, and if I didn't keep up, the grass would quickly become quite overgrown. No one else cared how anything looked, but I sure did, and I must admit that I was quite embarrassed to invite anybody to my home. When accepting a ride home from a classmate, most of the time I asked to be let off at the end of the driveway so they could not see how rundown the house was. Today, I would give anything to have that house back again and relish the memories it provided for me while growing up.

CHAPTER 5

Martha and Frank Kidd were very active in the Pentecostal church, yet I learned growing up in their household that the "practice what you preach" motto didn't necessarily apply. Since Martha was a preacher, and Frank was a deacon in the church, that should have meant no dancing, drinking, cussing, or smoking in our home. Well, that certainly was not the case as Martha swore like a sailor, and the two of them loved their unfiltered Pall Malls. We faithfully attended services every Wednesday, Thursday, Saturday, and twice on Sundays. During revivals, we went to church every night for a solid month. Our typical schedule was to come home from school, have dinner, do chores, and head to church. In fact, I did most of my homework in the pews of the church.

Despite her small size and shy nature, Martha had a robust presence in the church, and she would often preach the gospel with a voice that embodied the Almighty to me. She mostly preached during revivals, as many preachers from surrounding churches came with their congregations to give their sermons. There was much expected of us kids, and we were required by the Kidds to participate in many functions of the church. I was a part of the youth groups, where we often took field trips to other churches to hold game nights or organize picnics, and other social activities that were first approved by the deacon board.

I met most of my friends at church, which made sense considering we spent so much time together. Any play dates we were permitted to attend were scheduled between the end of Sunday school and before that evening's service. After Sunday school, I would head to my best friend's house to play games, ride bikes, or work on building car models, then have dinner before going back to church. I couldn't get dirty during these play dates because I had to go back to church in the same clothes that Sunday evening. This was a very safe way for Martha to permit us to have play dates, as the child welfare department was very strict at the time as to what foster children could and couldn't do. Playdates and sleepovers were forbidden for foster kids to participate in.

The Pentecostal religion in which we were raised is often referred to as the Holy Roller Church, mostly because a lot of shouting, dancing in the spirit, and speaking in tongues goes on during services and revivals. Revivals took place primarily in the summer months, held under a tent with folding chairs and a single podium. They would last anywhere from a week to two months, and people would come from all around the state to hear certain preachers preach. There would be songs to start, and most times they hosted guest singers as well. My sister and I were delighted to sing at many of these events. Two years later we were approached to record a gospel album, and we traveled from church to church singing almost every weekend. During these moments of praise through song, many people would shout, dance, and speak in tongues.

Speaking in tongues in the Pentecostal religion was considered a gift because it allowed you to speak directly to God. Sometimes there would be a message for the congregation in the language. Someone would speak while someone else would interpret the word. Often during these times, the spirit would come over Frank, and he would take off running around the church while praising Jesus at the top of his lungs. One of Frank's gifts was the gift of discernment, which is considered to be a Spirit-given ability to distinguish whether divine, human, or demonic origins are the source of what is present — whether it be in an atmosphere, encounter, event, or prophetic message. Frank would feel someone's pain, and when he said so aloud, the person feeling the pain would be encouraged to approach the altar to receive prayer. Most times the congregant would pass out under the spirit, only to get up moments later claiming that a miracle had just taken place.

Meanwhile, I would pray that the spirit would stay in Frank, hoping he would run at least four more laps around the church, which I calculated to equal a mile. Being into fitness and running, I wanted him to feel the same thing I experienced every time I ran. Also, I hoped that it would clean out his lungs from all those Pall Malls he smoked.

There were weekly services. There were revivals. There were youth groups. Yet across the board, the two primary topics most often repeated in the sermons were always about adultery and homosexuality. The congregation was told in no uncertain terms that anyone who committed such sins would be doomed to an eternity in Hell. We were told to avoid such a sentence, we must repent and ask for forgiveness, which required going to the altar where two elders would pray with us while we repented, saying, "Our

Heavenly Father, I ask you to forgive me of my sins." Once that was said, we were forgiven. As I grew older, I would find myself repenting all the time, mostly for my thoughts about the hot elders and my friends.

CHAPTER 6

When I was five years old, my brother, Jim, came to live with our group at Martha and Frank's farmhouse. Years earlier when we had been separated after leaving our mother's apartment, Jim had been taken to a children's home, where he was diagnosed with a slight case of mental retardation. He remained there until he was reunited with my sister and me at the Kidd's home. There was a stipulation at the time that children's homes could only house kids until they reached a certain age. Since Jim had turned sixteen, he had to leave.

It was great to have an older brother, even if he didn't look anything like me. He had strong features mixed with curious child-like expressions. He didn't take very good care of himself, and so his hygiene suffered. Most times he was half shaven and in dire need of a good shower. Yet, he so adored me and seemingly took great pride in boasting about me being his sibling. However, because of my young age, I experienced great embarrassment concerning his disheveled appearance and simple demeanor, in spite of how deeply I loved him.

My brother was a kind and gentle soul. He meant no harm to anyone and lived most of his short life in his own world. With what I believe to be his effort to connect with me in a brotherly way, he offered me the only gift he had to give, which was to teach me about sex. My brother was the first man to touch me sexually. I believe his outreach was out of pure affection for me as his younger brother. It was Jim's way of creating a bond to feel close to me. I think he may have known I was gay and wanted my first sexual experience to be a safe one.

At the age of seven, I was still not quite able to understand bodily functions. When Jim would bring me to his bed and show me how to play with him, I would then imitate those actions on myself. It left me feeling quite confused as I continuously misinterpreted his actions. His desire to show me affection was not sexual because sometimes I would take my penis out — randomly hoping to get attention — only to learn it was a secret and nobody should know what we did together. So I made sure that nobody did.

Unbeknownst to Jim, in keeping our activities a secret, I also learned shame. Like so many gay men, when our feelings are forced into secrecy, we learn that seeking validation through sex can often result in more shame. Something happened to me during those exchanges with my brother (that I now forgive), and it wasn't until many years later that I understood the purity of his intention.

When I was eight years old, Martha — knowing exactly what she was doing — sat me down to explain that I liked boys and that certain kinds of boys were going to like me back. She said that it was the unfortunate belief in the Pentecostal Church that "liking boys" and being gay would in no uncertain terms send me straight into the arms of Lucifer and his home of fire and brimstone in the depths of Hell. Like my secret with Jim, I understood the importance of keeping a secret, which in that case was that I was gay and liked boys. Also like my interactions with Jim, I identified with shame once again. I saw that labels can be created and that people can judge you and treat you differently.

Martha explained that it was essential that I keep the secret of my sexuality, and so I did. I repented all the time because of my thoughts and actions. The Lord heard about my desire to kiss a boy, to fit in, and that I desired to be liked by a boy. He heard how I often stared at the Gilmore brothers in awe of their physical beauty. He also heard that I got in trouble for not taking out the trash, or that I broke a lamp. Some very simple things were shameful for me at the time.

CHAPTER 7

Initially, Paul and Lenore were permitted to visit my sister, Jim, and me on holidays. Being the accidental child as well as a constant reminder to Lenore of how I was conceived, I was not favored during any of these visits. Fully aware of what she was doing, Lenore showered my brother and sister with beautifully wrapped packages, while my gifts were delivered in used brown paper bags or bundled in last week's dirty newspaper. My siblings received fashionable new clothing and the latest toys. I always received ill-fitting and mismatched second-hand clothes that needed repair or unboxed board games with missing pieces. If Lenore was feeling generous, she might gift me with a fractured representation of what was once some child's precious toy. Somehow — using the strength I developed in those weeks when I was uncared for in my crib — I was able to set aside the hurt and embarrassment and accept Lenore's gifts graciously.

The visits were stopped when I was eight years old, which allowed Lenore one final Christmas with us. True to form, she arrived with gifts aplenty. My sister received a beautiful Victorian doll pristinely wrapped in crinkle paper and adorned with festive holiday silver, gold, blue, green, and red ribbons and bows. My brother exuberantly unwrapped a new train set complete with tracks, a caboose, and a miniature snow-sprinkled New England village. Holding back tears, and fearful of what might happen, I cautiously opened my gift and hoped that what I would find inside would at least be something new. Inside a brown paper bag, I discovered a Dixie cup full of melted wax, and a charcoaled wick with the artificial floral scent of bathroom daisies. Clearly, my gift had once been a candle. As I had done so many times before, I said, "Thank you, it's what I've always wanted." That was the last visit that Martha would permit, thankfully.

When I was ten years old, I no longer received a new clothing allowance from the state. This was not a regular occurrence, but a way for the child welfare department to meet budget. There seemed to be no regard for the psychological damage it would cause foster children to not be assisted with such basic necessities. In spite of my young age, it became my responsibility to earn money to pay for my own clothing. I felt I needed to do so to not only help Martha but to make sure my needs were met as a budding fashion-minded gay boy.

When the welfare department appointed me to be the janitor at my elementary school, it was presented as though I was being given a gift or an opportunity that was only awarded to a lucky, chosen few. So it was that at the age of ten, I fully realized that I was underprivileged — which caused me to feel both embarrassed and ashamed. These two feelings I felt so often in my life that for too many years they became synonymous with the way I functioned in the world.

After school, I hid in the lockers until my friends had gone home and the school was empty of students. Then I began my responsibilities as a 10-year-old in the work world. I swept the floors, scraped the gum from the chairs that I had watched my friends chew earlier in the day, mopped the steps, cleaned the windows, wiped down the chalkboards, and every other day I scrubbed the toilets. I didn't mind the actual work, as that was the easy part. The infinitely more difficult part was realizing that I was different — that I lived on the poor side of the tracks, and that I was more or less alone in the world.

Every morning upon my arrival at school, I entered the office, and the secretary handed me a small yellow ticket for a free meal. It was a form of food stamps, and I would shamefully put the ticket into my pocket. I could almost feel it burning a hole in my pants as I was reminded of my position in life. The yellow ticket not only represented my free lunch but the possibility of pending doom that my poverty could be revealed in front of my classmates.

As I stood in the cafeteria line for lunch each day, I would experience great anxiety as I rounded the bend at the dessert counter. I didn't know who the cashier ladies would be from day to day. Once I spotted them, I quickly positioned myself in the line with whomever I perceived to be the most discreet yellow ticket taker, knowing I would hand her my ticket to her in front of all the other kids in line. Some ladies would quietly take the ticket with no one seeing, but others would call out so everyone would know I got a free lunch, "I got another yellow-ticket kid here. WELFARE LUNCH!"

CHAPTER 8

Despite — or perhaps because of — the challenges I navigated as a foster child, I had two things in my life that I could always depend upon to keep me going: singing and exercise. I had a lot of energy, and while some might have called me "loud," I always preferred the word "vocal." The simple truth was that singing was a way for me to heal the daily emotional assaults that peppered me. I first began singing in the church choir and continued when I wasn't in church. Whenever I sang, any troubles or anxiety disappeared for me, as singing helped me get through any situation. I sang mostly church songs when I was young. As I grew older, I would sing a lot of James Taylor and inspirational songs from movies. Every song I sang resonated hope and the ability to dream.

I was just seven years old when I first started lifting cement blocks, paint cans, and bales of hay to facilitate my fledgling workouts. I found it to be great fun to stretch my body and grow in those ways, and those early experiences created a lifetime love of exercise. But it was really my daily runs that produced the spaces for me to feel truly happy. Running provided a significant release of bottled-up anger for me, a channel to release that toxic sludge that so easily accumulated. Exercise became my saving grace in neutralizing my emotions.

I was a little guy, and I wanted to become stronger so my farming chores would be easier for me to do. I knew I needed to build my strength, as lifting bales of hay on a daily basis became a struggle I was determined to overcome. After months of saving my allowance, I had enough money to send for an exercise program I found on the back of a magazine. While knowing that the money should go to something I had to have — such as clothes — I secretly sent away for the program anyway. For my investment, I received twelve issues, one per month. Each issue was filled with how-to exercises demonstrated by sketches of bodybuilding hunks — a benefit I eagerly looked forward to with each mailing. Some exercises required weights, which I didn't have, so I used anything I could substitute on the farm.

My favorite part of exercise and perhaps my most dangerous secret was the way I finished my daily run. I raced up the massive hill that led down into a valley before going over a smaller hill to my driveway. As I reached the top of the bigger hill, I would sometimes find myself feeling overwhelmed by the possibilities of being kidnapped or seduced, things I found both thrilling and incredibly frightening. Many of my childhood thoughts, fears, experiences, and fantasies presented themselves in the valley as I ran home. Some were scary, such as parked cars with older men waiting inside to request sexual favors. Some were exciting, such as increasing my time or challenging myself to go harder. Some were forbidden, such as when I stopped to interact with mixed outcomes. Those were my beautiful, terrifying, and often life-changing childhood dreams created while running up and down country hills. I had dreams of being the best athlete, the greatest teacher, or maybe a doctor. No matter what it might be, it was always a way for me to become a better person than I was at the time. To always think of a way out of whatever troubled me. They were all life-defining through experience while providing me with a clearer vision of who I wanted to be and who I chose not to be. Every time I visit Ohio, I return to those hills, take a run, and remember.

Once I reached the smaller hill and was closer to home, I would often imagine that as I raced down the hill toward the mailbox, I would be greeted by crowds of people on either side of the road saying my name in harmony, cheering me on to the finish line. That represented pure and unadulterated love to me. Incidentally, many years later that dream came to fruition. During my first Los Angeles Marathon, as I approached mile 25 of the 26.2-mile finish line, I started running faster, conjuring up the memories of running through the valley. This time there actually were thousands of people roaring in support on both sides of the street, cheering my name in the most glorious harmonics that as a child I could have never imagined. As I crossed that finish line, it was truly a magical moment I will always remember. Dreams do come true.

CHAPTER 9

It was in junior high that I began to experience progressively deeper depths of shame. I was mercilessly bullied, threatened, name-called, and reminded on a daily basis that I lived on "the other side of the tracks." My voice was high pitched, and I hung out with girls — two things that drew several bullies to me like magnets, despite what I did to escape their notice. I would be shoved down the steps with a strong hand to my back. My books would be knocked from my hands. Any book reports or presentations were ruined before I could show them to my classmates. I was made fun of in class. Gum was put on my seat. Spit wads were shot at my head.

I spent lots of time hiding in lockers after school until the bullies were gone. I had very few male friends in school and would spend hours praying that some guy would like me and want to be my friend. My junior high years were agonizing for me. I lived deep in a well of shame, and my secrets were crippling as I struggled about how to grow into a young man. Living my guarded gay life, I continually tried to find people I could like and who might like me back, but I never quite fit in. I definitely marched to a colorful and wildly different beat in that small town of Wadsworth, Ohio. It would take me years to realize that the colors I at first wore with shame would become the rainbow from which I would slide into my pot of gold.

I never invited anybody from school to my house because I felt it was too run-down and I was embarrassed and ashamed of what my classmates would think. The friends I did have were from my church; however, I never came out to them and told them the truth about my sexuality. I lived in fear of their righteous and judgmental God-fearing persecution. Not only making friends but keeping them was a real struggle for me. It was much easier to be alone, so I spent much of my time in my own company and much enjoyed it. Since I lived on a farm with chickens, cows, pigs, and horses, they became my company, and that's why I love the book *Charlotte's Web* to this day.

Once in high school, I became even more aware that I was different. And so did everyone else. While it would have been easy for me to seek refuge in drugs and alcohol, thank goodness my overachieving desire to please kept me safe. I would never take a misstep as I knew that any poor choice on my end could result in my removal from the child services department and placement in a juvenile detention center. I wasn't willing to take such a risk, so I invested a lot of time and energy into performing as best as I could.

Several times per week I visited the office of Mr. Parsons, my guidance counselor. He believed in me and encouraged me to be the best I could be, no matter what. I still call him on Father's Day to thank him for all that he did for me during those troubling and confusing times. It was then, and as a result of his support that I began to embrace my differences as part of who I really was. For example, because I knew how to sew, I made alterations to my clothes as well as created new outfits that would represent my colorful life choices. I became brave enough to wear whatever made me feel good. Clogs and hip huggers were the most fashionable, so of course, I purchased both with the money I made as a school janitor.

When I started to wrestle, I subsequently made some great friends. As per the usual, I worked very hard to please my wrestling coach, and I excelled in everything else that I did. I was very active in school overall: I wrestled, ran track, pole vaulted, practiced gymnastics, and was the school mascot all throughout my school years. After school, I would go to practice for two hours, then assume my duties as the school janitor. I worked until the floors were immaculate, the chalkboards washed, the bathrooms scrubbed, the gum scraped from under every seat, along with a multitude of other responsibilities before walking the five miles home each night.

When I was a junior in high school, I finally discovered a distraction tactic to battle my bullies: I learned how to make them laugh. I auditioned for our school production of Barefoot in the Park by Neil Simon and landed a part as the telephone repairman. As it was a character role, it was one in which I could be funny. I loved making the audience laugh, and received excellent reviews for my performances. I was also a star wrestler at the time, so the two commitments conflicted. I decided not to wrestle and to perform in the play instead. That decision started a chain reaction of bullying from my coach, teachers, and classmates. I was often asked to stay after school to be lectured and reminded of where I came from. These lectures were invariably designed to break me down and then bully me into a sport or an activity I had already chosen not to do. It was a very tough year, but I loved the play and was so grateful for the opportunity to perform.

During my senior year, I had a life-changing and serendipitous moment: I met a man. I had applied for a student teaching position, and Bill chose me to be his student teacher for part of my senior year. Bill set an example for me that I needed at that time of my life more than I even realized. Sequestered in that small town as I was, Bill was more than a breath of fresh air — he was a tornado of excitement and change for me. An over-the-top Aqua Net blonde, who was flamboyant, immaculately dressed, hyper affected, ahead of his time — Bill was a flaming out-of-the-closet homosexual. He embraced every part of himself and was wide open about who and what he was. He was brilliant, articulate, and immensely creative, and by taking me under his wing, he consequently taught me much about life as a young gay man. Bill set a powerful example for me to begin my greatest journey on how to understand myself and the world around me. I had very little instruction from my foster father Frank about how to become a man, so I didn't have a role model to look up to until I met Bill.

Until that point, I kept a journal where I wrote about the different kinds of men who passed through my life. I carefully observed them, taking note of their different behaviors, and noting the characteristics that I liked — as well as the ones I didn't. I loved men who were smart and clean-cut, well-spoken, and who dressed well. They were funny and also took good care of themselves. I watched their every movement, such as how they acted around other men, children, and women. Then I picked and chose the qualities I wanted and incorporated them into my life.

That journal was my most precious secret, and it was carefully guarded. I kept it under my bed in a locked, wooden box.

Using the notes I wrote those many years ago was ultimately responsible for crafting me into the person I am today. I learned to be kind and loving towards others — to appreciate the joy of giving, as well as receiving. I saw the importance of appreciating my body and how to take care of it through exercise and good grooming. I learned how to respect myself, as well as others. I learned to work through anger and disagreements in learning how to love and receive love. I appreciated the importance of working hard and enjoying life. Thanks to all of those men who passed through my life in my earlier years, I didn't travel my journey of growth and discovery alone.

CHAPTER 10

During the latter part of my high school years, like many times before, I was introduced to yet another social worker. To most other social workers, I was just a name or a number, and usually, they only lasted a couple years in the field at the most. But Cathy was different. She had just graduated from college and was young, idealistic, and full of love and energy. Most importantly for me, Cathy was very interested in me and my future. When she asked me if there was one thing I could wish for, I answered without hesitation that I wanted to go to college.

Cathy went to Columbus Ohio to rally for me to receive a Pell Grant. She went because she was genuinely invested in making my future the best it could be, and she saw where she could make the most significant impact. The Pell Grant allows foster kids who are considered wards of the state to go to college and helps them with tuition and housing. The application process was overwhelming, to say the least, as my emotions and self-doubt were all over the place. What if they didn't accept me? What if we did all this work for nothing? Every possible scenario ran through my mind as I turned each page of the massive application. Cathy helped me get the Pell grant by adding kids who were wards of the state to the application process.

I chose to attend Kent State University for a couple of reasons. First, Bill — the influential teacher I had assisted in high school — had attended Kent State. Secondly, the university was one of the only schools that accepted wards of the state. And finally, Kent State was almost in financial ruin due to what came to be called the Kent State Massacre. Four university students had been killed, and nine were injured on May 4, 1970, when members of the Ohio National Guard opened fire on a crowd gathered to protest the Vietnam War. In the aftermath of the killings, a student-led strike forced the temporary closure of colleges and universities across the country. As it was just a couple of years after the infamous protest and shooting over the Vietnam war outrage, the campus was still quite barren. There were only two dorms open at the time, one for girls and one for boys.

I moved into the dorm by myself. Although Martha and Frank were supportive in their own way, they really had no concept of college or higher education. It is unlikely they understood just how incredible it was that I was able to attend college at all, considering my early beginning. I was scared but very excited to embark on this unknown journey. However, I quickly met new people and started forming what would become my college family. The state of Ohio paid for everything except my books but made it possible for me to work on campus. My first job (ironically) was a cafeteria food server, which lasted for several weeks. While I loved the job, I was told that I served oversized portions (no irony lost there). I was subsequently released from my duties without notice because my repeated mantra of "enjoy your meal" apparently annoyed the other students.

Most jobs were usually assigned to students before the quarter began, and my situation was unique in that I was required to have a job to receive the grant money. When I was released from being a cafeteria server, I approached the Intramural sports department. Although there wasn't a job available, the director of the department created a special position for me, which was to monitor four young ladies who met in a small room on Tuesdays and Thursdays to "exercise." These overly ambitious young women had no idea how to exercise correctly, and for a couple of days, I watched them show up just to move around and gossip.

After watching their interactions for a bit, I brought in my disco albums which included Donna Summer, Sylvester, and the pièce de résistance — Saturday Night Fever. Instant hit! The young ladies loved it, and soon we were dancing, laughing, and expressing our emotions through movement and exercise. The next time we met, my four ladies each brought a friend and our class instantly doubled to eight. It didn't stop there, for once the word got out that there was a class on campus that could be fun, challenging, and beneficial to your health, the attendees kept on coming. Soon my reputation preceded me, and that's how my class was named, "Get Slim with Tim." When the number of ladies exceeded our space, we were moved into the new gym with expandable rooms. By the time I was a senior, more than 4,000 women were attending my classes.

In addition to teaching every Tuesday and Thursday, I also became a gymnast and cheerleader. I cheered throughout the four years of my college experience, becoming the captain in my junior and senior years. Our team competed each year, and we won first place three out of the four years. We were in a smaller division then, but I went on after college to become a professional cheerleader when I traveled the country teaching camps and cheering for teams during the Cotton Bowl, Fiesta Bowl, and Orange Bowl. It was great fun!

CHAPTER 11

I loved college. I found a new level of freedom, as well as a delicious sense of belonging. For the first time in my life, I truly understood and grasped the full potential and opportunity for me to be anything I wanted to be. It was terrifically liberating to not only finally find a place where I belonged but to take a hand in creating that environment for myself. I formed life-long friendships during those years, and It was during that time that my truth as a gay man fully and safely emerged. Kent State, in spite of being in Ohio, was extremely progressive at that time and I made lots of gay friends — people who were like me. People who understood me. We regularly socialized together, frequenting the downtown discos to the sounds of Donna Summer, Sylvester, the Weather Sisters, and Anita Ward, to name a few. Donna Summer was everything to me as her music lifted me to such levels of happiness. To this day, dancing is one of my favorite forms of expression.

In fact, it was during the last semester of my sophomore year while I was out dancing with my friends that I met Bob. He was eleven years older than me, and already very established in his career while I was at that time still a fun-loving college kid with two pairs of shorts and three T-shirts. I was enamored by Bob's high style, and

I soon went from wearing Fruit of the Loom to Polo, greatly enjoying my "moment of snobbery." However, my friends did their best to bring me back to reality, a reality that would stay with me and keep me in check throughout my college years. That humility guided me into perhaps what would become my most genuine and most honest moment. I was very recognizable on campus and attended great parties. The one fantastic benefit from being so identifiable was that I was nominated and crowned Kent State's Homecoming King in my senior year. Before 1981 at Kent State University, there had never been an openly gay, demonstratively colorful, pre-gay pride, rainbow-wearing Homecoming King. It was a humbling and genuinely unexpected honor that I would share with Bob. He actually came to the game and watched me be crowned. He didn't stay for the festivities, but it meant a lot to have his support.

Bob was the first man that I loved. He was like no one I had ever known at that point, and perhaps it was his novelty that I found so appealing. For example, he was the vice president of a major hotel chain, New England born and raised, and well-accustomed to a very unique lifestyle. We could not have been more different. Bob showered me with presents, including my first car: a maroon Oldsmobile Cutlass Supreme T-top. I had never been treated that way before by anybody, and it was absolutely intoxicating.

Unbeknownst to me, Bob was grooming me to be his arm candy. I didn't know what arm candy was, and I always wanted to believe that he loved me. I loved Bob without reserve and refused to accept any rumors that I was anything less than his equal partner. A great many of his friends were much older than me and would make offensive comments about how I dressed, acted, and spoke. As time went on, Bob became possessive of every move I made. It didn't bother me at first — because it felt to me as though he acted in particular ways because he really cared for me.

When I graduated from Kent State University with a BS in science, double majoring in physical education and dance, I was offered scholarships to the University of Southern California and New York University. Bob took an active hand in guiding my future and manipulated me into choosing NYU. I would never discover the truth behind a rather ominous statement he made, which was, "You can go anywhere in the world, but not Los Angeles." So, New York it was, which was a momentous change for me.

When I arrived in New York City, at heart, I was still a young, relatively innocent country boy. I had been very sheltered growing up in Wadsworth and had minimal experience with travel or big cities. I was in shock in going from the lush, wide-open green spaces of Ohio to New York's 1980's concrete jungle. For the first time in my life, I saw a homeless person. It was a traumatic experience for me to witness a person asking for money because he was hungry. I called Martha and asked what I should do. Her reply was so honest and pure, and I follow her advice to this day. She said, "Make sure he has water and a sandwich."

It was quite an adjustment for me to spend extended periods of time alone in a big city. I didn't get to branch out as much as I should have because I was worried about what Bob would think, which was a bit tragic because I was in the thick of New York's gay movement. The Stonewall Riot of 1969 was the first significant incident in which gay men took a collective and forceful stand against police brutality.

The development of the gay community and fighting back became a catalyst for the sexual revolution, which then gave way to disco fever. I did go to Studio 54, where I danced with Andy Warhol and Bianca Jagger. And when Donna Summer came out of the ceiling singing her latest hit, "Last Dance" I really thought I'd died and gone to heaven.

The 1980s New York disco scene was laden with drugs. In particular, piles of coke and Quaaludes and poppers were the rage. The crazier the better as the norm shifted from trend followers to people who couldn't care less about what everyone else was doing. I was just another one of the young people embracing the new-found freedom to the fullest. It was "in" to be seen, loved, picked up, drugged, and be who you felt like being. The disco clubs of that pre-AIDS era created spaces for us to explore sexuality and self-expression.

After the discos closed, we'd head to the Pink Flamingo, which was the after-bar at the time. I remember thinking, "Wow! This place serves breakfast in the disco!" While staying out all night for days on end was the norm at the time, I only got to observe and be entertained. I always had a client or a class to teach early in the morning and had to be on my game. I couldn't afford to be hungover or high for my obligations.

Fire Island, the large center island of the outer barrier islands parallel to Long Island, was the place to be during those hot summers. It was post-Stonewall, pre-AIDS, and being gay was the norm. I have fond memories of taking a house with friends and dancing until the sun came up. But unfortunately, I only got to go a couple of times because Bob insisted on taking a house in the Hamptons instead.

That was a much calmer vibe with wealthy, stuffy, gay men.

I lived in the dorm during my college years in New York and then moved in with Bob after I graduated when he traded his position in Cleveland for one in New York. He traveled a lot, and I started working for a fitness studio. At the time, I was also a professional cheerleader, and I went around the country teaching cheerleading camps. I much enjoyed traveling about to see different places and meet all kinds of new people. I got to experience different cultures and traditions through the many festivals and county fairs we attended as guests.

The fly in the ointment was that Bob became increasingly possessive and suspicious, and because we were spending so much time apart, he continually accused me of cheating on him. I never cheated on Bob, but his continuing accusations wore me down. I was in Georgia teaching at a cheerleading camp when something snapped. I reached my limit. I decided not to return to New York and purchased a one-way ticket to Los Angeles.

I wanted to be where fitness started, and Los Angeles was known for being the best of everything when it came to fitness. Although Bob was extremely unhappy and fought me on my decision, he ultimately accepted that our relationship was over. In truth, our relationship had become more father/son than partner/lover. With time, we established an enduring friendship and remained quite close until Bob passed.

CHAPTER 12

I arrived in Los Angeles in early 1983 with $150 in my pocket and a bag in each hand. The first thing I did was rent a car for two weeks from a place aptly named Rent-a-Wreck for $18 a day. Then I took a small room for a week at the tiny Tropicana hotel on Santa Monica Boulevard. At McDonald's, I played every game I could in an attempt to win a free meal and I always won at least one meal a day. My new life was a far cry from the safety and comfort of Bob, and I spent most of that first week crying, thinking about what a colossal mistake I'd made.

Once I was finished feeling sorry for myself, I knew I needed to find a gym, so I walked across the street from the motel and saw that a gym was just about to open. I walked inside just as another guy walked out shouting that he quit. I spoke up to the owner and said without hesitation that I would take that guy's front counter job. Soon I was greeting clients, explaining the rules, and managing the towels and memberships. It was the perfect way for me to meet new people and make friends.

The time I could afford at the Tropicana Motel came to an end, so I took to sleeping in my rental car in the parking lot of a Ralphs supermarket. I washed my hair in a nearby pizza restaurant. In spite of that inconvenience, dirty hair was just not an option, and I did whatever it took to maintain the high standards of my personal hygiene. My daily life was shockingly different from when I had been living with Bob. But since I grew up with very little, I knew I could make do and do whatever it took to survive. When I showed up to work with car seat lines etched on my face, my manager — puzzled by what was usually my impeccable appearance — asked me what was going on. I confessed that I'd been sleeping in my car but not to worry as it was a rental and I could only afford it for one more day. Flabbergasted, he offered his couch to me for a month and found me a bike to ride.

Eternally grateful, every day I rode my bike six miles through heavy traffic from Westwood to West Hollywood until I eventually landed in West Hollywood in a single apartment that I so loved. I rode that bike for the first six years I lived in Los Angeles. When I could finally afford a moped, I drove it for the next eight years until I could afford to buy a car. I paid $3,000 for a blue Chevy Cavalier that literally had been owned by a little old lady from Pasadena.

I had been at the gym for about two weeks when a trainer approached me to say he was leaving the state and asked if I would be interested in taking his clients to train. He said he thought I would be a great personal trainer considering my qualifications. I was probably even a little overqualified with a BS degree from Kent State in Kinesiology, another degree from NYU in rehabilitation medicine, and a further degree from UCLA in physiology and functional movement. It was clearly an excellent fit for me at the time, and I gratefully accepted his generous offer.

As luck would have it, my first client was the infamous Richard Simmons. I rode my bike to his place off of Sunset Plaza Drive and up into the glamorous, star-studded hills of Hollywood. Richard and I were very similar in nature, and so we got along quite well, as both of us exuberantly expressed our journeys through life. After several years of training together, we wrote a book and created exercise videos. During those years Richard was also shooting his morning show. I became Richard's "shadow." Most celebrities creating exercise videos at the time had a shadow whose job it was to choreograph and create the exercises for them. Inadvertently, it was through my shadow work with Richard that my own path became clear.

Eventually, I would come to be recognized as an elite trainer to the stars, celebrities, and billionaires. For the next 37 years, I would travel the world with my high-profile clients, living a lifestyle that most foster kids could only dream about.

CHAPTER 13

It was 1983–1984 and Los Angeles was not only the place to be but most definitely the place for me. I loved my life and felt at the time that I'd genuinely hit my stride. Nothing could stop me! My earlier struggles in life fell into my rear-view mirror as I began crafting the life for myself that I had always wanted.

I had a good number of friends. I had a place of my own. I was teaching exercise and enjoying an outrageous number of followers. It was indeed a magical time. Most wonderful was that I became connected to a fabulous group of 40 guys who worked out at the gym at differing times. We did everything together, enjoying a variety of activities including dinners, parties, beach days, theater, and fundraisers. We traveled to Laguna, San Diego, and San Francisco. We camped in Big Bear or in someone's backyard. We celebrated every holiday together in one form or another. My days of feeling alone and misunderstood were over as I reveled in the fact that I had created my Los Angeles family.

Billy was the manager at the gym and very much the central figure of our group. Standing 5'8", he was the typical surfer boy in appearance, with blond hair, blue eyes, and a smile that could bring you to your knees. He was the group's social guru, organizing the trips, the parties, and the special events that we participated in. Billy was the one who not only gave me a place to stay, a bike on which to get around but also made sure I was eating. He routinely checked in with me to make sure I was doing well. I felt he genuinely cared for me, and naturally, I cared very much for him as well. Billy was an extraordinary man and a very dear friend to me.

While there were many wonderful and undoubtedly quite handsome men in the group, I became especially fond of Roy. While he stood 6'3", Roy had very skinny legs that he worked on endlessly at the gym — to no avail. While he was fortunate to have a beautiful chest, abs, and well-defined arms, his back and butt were always in need of exercise. He was pigeon-toed and had a slight limp when he walked.

Roy was a talented and accomplished carpenter and cabinet maker, as well as a heart-centered, well-intentioned sex worker. He worked as a part-time escort, and his client base (or his little black book) consisted of high-end clergy, city officials, and rockstar listings. He also had a long-time partner named Joe who worked as a coroner, of all things. Although complicated, they had an open relationship, and that suited me quite well for what I needed at the time. Roy and I were soon inseparable, and with Joe's blessings, we spent much of our time together. We truly loved each other, but unfortunately for me, it was conditional in that our relationship required my understanding and acceptance of his other interests. Yet our relationship functioned very well within the group, and I felt truly blessed in loving, being loved by, and enjoying the companionship of so many exceptional men.

Then there was that fateful day when I received a call that Billy had inexplicably been checked into the hospital. I reached out to our group of friends and four of us headed to the hospital to see what was going on. None of our friends had any idea what was wrong with Billy. It was very frightening when we realized that no one at the hospital seemed to know what exactly was wrong with our friend either. When we arrived, we were told that we needed to dress in head coverings, special shirts, pants, coverings for our shoes, and we had to wear masks. Since Billy was the closest to a brother any one of us could ever have imagined, collectively we decided not to wear the prescribed "costumes." We chose to be present in our brother-loving natural state for Billy. The staff was at first horrified and insisted that we were putting ourselves in grave danger. As our support for Billy became apparent, they eventually stopped their remonstrations. A very few became supportive.

When we were finally permitted to enter Billy's hospital room, we were beyond horrified to see the conditions in which Billy was living. Food trays were piled floor-to-ceiling against the wall. Dirty bedding was discarded in the corners. The bathroom by any standards would have been condemned. And if his physical surroundings weren't heartbreaking enough, Billy himself was weak, disoriented, and neglected. It was clear to the four of us that no one had attended to the room or to Billy for fear of being infected by his unknown illness. This was a hysterical diagnosis of the time, but sadly, probably not all that unusual.

Nevertheless, we pushed our sleeves up to our elbows, told hospital staff to stay out of our way, and together we cleaned his room. We bathed our dear brother Billy's emaciated body with loving care through our tears, fears, and compassion. Unfortunately, by this point Billy was delusional. He cried about the monsters, spiders, and snakes crawling along the hospital walls. But those times when he was present were met with love and total reassurance that we were there and we would always be until he took his last breath.

A couple of days later we were told he had what they were describing at the time as "the gay disease." Of course, the medical community would soon identify that disease as Acquired Immune Deficiency Syndrome, or AIDS. I'm not sure how Billy became infected but the strain he had was incredibly strong, and he died within two weeks of entering the hospital.

At first, the disease was diagnosed as a form of pneumonia. But when the CDC noted that the first cases were all in homosexual men, fear began to spread. There was an extreme uncertainty that surrounded the disease at the early stage. Even finding a name for the illness was challenging, and so it was first called "gay-related immune deficiency," or GRID, but the name was changed when it was discovered that heterosexuals could also be infected. Even after more was known about the disease (including modes of transmission), the outside world exploded in fear and ignorance. In the 1980s, "AIDS hysteria" became a familiar term.

For my close friends and me, that initial visit to Billy was the beginning of a very dark and devastating period of time. I watched every single one of my close friends, as well as more than 850 men in my gym, die over a ten-year period. There was Joey, the most talented seamstress in the world, who also happened to be a very decorated beauty queen. Keith was one of the greatest artists of our time. Brian had a voice that one could only wish for, and when I heard him sing in several operas I was always reduced to tears. Sam could at any time pick up any instrument and play the most fantastic music. Joshua's legs could reach the sky when he danced. He had just been accepted into the Alvin Ailey American Dance Theater right before the disease ravaged his body. Many teachers, police officers, firefighters, nurses, doctors, store clerks, and CEOs passed away. AIDS knew no boundaries.

In 1984 there were 7,239 cases of AIDS reported to date and 5,596 deaths. By the end of 1985, AIDS had been reported in 51 countries and on every continent except Antarctica. Rock Hudson died of AIDS that year, and 15,527 cases of AIDS were reported, along with 12,529 deaths. For the next several years, the number doubled and doubled. I did not need to be informed of those numbers because I watched it happen. Every single man in my group of forty passed, one by one. The dinner parties, weekend excursions, and holiday celebrations thinned until there just weren't enough of us left who felt like celebrating. Of our original group, only Roy, Joe, and I survived that initial wave of death. At the peak, I attended two to three memorial services a day, eventually becoming so numb to death that I had little emotion left.

Oddly enough, attending those memorial services actually became a strange social outlet to meet new people. Attending funerals several times a day had us all running into the same guys over and over. Yet it was a devastating and desperate time during those 15 years of watching talented young men in the prime of their lives pass while knowing it could be me at any moment. Grief-stricken, we each grasped for ways to understand the cosmic disorder and unnatural realization of what was happening to our loved ones. Those of us who survived the "plague" (hetero-normative description) reached out to each other for comfort as if in a sacred tribal ceremony. Together, we moaned to the heavens, not understanding the rhyme nor reason behind the devastation of an entire culture. It was truly beyond our comprehension.

CHAPTER 14

Several drugs quickly became available. Many of the first drug trials failed to help at all or merely prolonged the inevitable and painful decline AIDS caused for its victims. The drugs were toxic and had many devastating side effects such as hair loss, aging to the point of nonrecognition, misshapen and swollen belly, painful joints, total numbness in different parts of the body, constant vomiting, diarrhea 24/7, loss of sight and movement, hallucinations, and finally night sweats.

There was significant panic throughout the world about the disease, and if you were infected, you were forever marked. I watched men agree to use their bodies as battlegrounds for testing as the medical communities fought, lied, and deceived us. I watched as many of my friends decided to take up to one hundred and fifty pills three times a day with the blind hope that they would at least be able to get out of bed. I witnessed the results of these unknown combinations decimate what was left of my community. For some reason I still can't explain, I said no to the experimental medication. Instead, I threw myself into work by exercising, teaching, and competing in aerobic championships. I wanted to stay in control of my body as long as I could, even if in the back of my mind I was willing to accept the unexpected. It was a very tragic time for me to watch everything I had so joyfully built crumble all around me. Once again, I felt helpless and abandoned as circumstances outside my control devastated my life.

Several years later, the Center for Disease Control released a test we could take to see if we were HIV positive, or if we had full-blown AIDS. UCLA started a men's group where we could go every three months to give blood, urine, sperm, and saliva. They kept records of our vital statistics and compared them after each visit. I was one of the first to go with Roy. At that point I'd already accepted the fact that I must have been infected, based on how many men in our group I'd been sexual with had passed away. When we received our results, I wasn't surprised. Roy and I both had been infected with the virus and naturally so had Joe.

By that point, we were just waiting to see how long it would be before something happened to us. I had prepared myself for death. I was ready to go ... and yet nothing happened. I continually questioned why I wasn't yet dead. Why was I still alive when nearly all of my friends and lovers were gone? I honestly never thought I would see the age of forty. It just didn't seem possible that I continued to live. Once again I found myself in that familiar space of keeping another secret. It would be twenty years before I told anyone that I had tested positive. Instead, I just pretended my status wasn't of any consequence and continued living my life in the ways that I chose. By that time, I had become very good at compartmentalizing every aspect of my life. No one knew the authentic me. I allowed others to perceive me in ways in which I remained firmly in control.

I maintained a fierce veneer as a trainer and an aerobics instructor. Teaching aerobics in those days was like how cheerleading had been for me in college: it became the only thing that could genuinely brighten my day. But it also enabled my strong desire to hide: as long as I remained high on enthusiasm no one would know how I felt inside. Or so I thought. I taught three to five high-impact classes a day. My classes were so popular that aerobics competitions popped up everywhere. To me, these competitions were like a cheerleading routine put to music. It was a great distraction for me during those dark days.

Over the ten years, I competed in many aerobics competitions, from the local level to regional, state, and finally national. The competitions were always sponsored by companies like Reebok and Coppertone, and people came from all over to try out. Only the top three were chosen. In individual men and women's mixed pairs and trios, I won seven major titles, as well as over 15–20 local, regional, state, and national titles. The prizes ranged from a new car, a cruise or cash prizes from $15–$25,000.

With one of my wins, I opened the first private gym in West Hollywood. While today there are more than one hundred private gyms within a ten-mile radius, no one thought a private gym would be successful back then. But it was. I had at least five trainers training at all times, a front desk attendant, and valet parking. I had it decorated with dark green carpeting and white machines. I put all of my energy into the gym, pouring every bit of my emotional and physical fuel into it. I showed people an image of perfection I wanted them to see. It was a hefty burden for me to bear for as long as I did, because in addition to running the gym, and training celebrities, I was still teaching aerobics.

No one could imagine, let alone believe, the secrets I was keeping beneath my stoic veneer. I did not disclose to anyone my thoughts or fears about my health, sadness, grief, and missing those I lost, as well as the fear of losing the gym. I showed none of this to anyone else.

In addition to my three other careers, I started a school to certify trainers, to help them get started in the business, as well as teach them how to maintain a substantial clientele. I taught my beloved Roy to become a personal trainer, and he eventually opened his own gym, too.

Despite the initial devastation of losing swaths of friends and discovering my own positive status, everything in my life was going well for about a year. Then I received the most terrible of news: my best friend, lover, confidant, and the only man who truly knew me confessed that the disease had taken over his brain. Doctors told Roy he had only months to live. We had been together at least fourteen years at that point, and the thought of life without Roy was simply incomprehensible.

Naturally, Joe knew as well and was ready to put together a plan for us. Little did we know that Joe was actually the sicker one and would go before Roy.

CHAPTER 15

With this devastating news, I imploded.

Every single thing that I had painstakingly created and designed — my persona, dedication to endless and unwavering potential for greatness, and boundless levels and exuberant enthusiasm for life — came to a screeching halt. Also, all the sadness and grief that I had stuffed inside during those many years spent helplessly watching my close friends die came roaring to the surface. That experience was like nothing I had ever known before. Despite transcending some tough times in my past, I felt lost, confused, and so terribly alone. When that avalanche of emotions, crumbling facades, and truths all collided, I knew enough to know that I couldn't do it by myself. I needed help. I found a guy who was beginning his career as a therapist and just starting his internship. We immediately got along and together we started a 10 to 15-year journey of healing and discovery that lasted until he got his Ph.D.

Therapy saved my life, of that I have no doubt. Although it was very hard at first to deal with and face my deep sorrow, I persevered. Awareness, acceptance, and the desire to change and follow through were vital tools I had to develop. I spent many hours in his office over the years melting into deep rivers of crying, crying, and crying over the hard times. With his help, I was eventually able to assemble the tools that I needed to become the whole of me and not just compartmentalized versions at designated times. I not only talked about and discovered these things in therapy, but, each time, I was given homework to utilize what I had learned with people I trusted at first, and then to make more bolder moves and choices with strangers. Slowly, I became a person with an awareness of what it meant to be in touch with all parts of who I was, instead of just for the sake of protection or affection. That was a momentous undertaking, and one I am proud to have accomplished.

Entering therapy when I did enabled me to take on the challenging job of becoming Roy's caretaker. Sadly, Roy's family had joined a cult in rebellion to the AIDS epidemic and informed him that they wanted nothing to do with him. Since he shared a fantastic house with Joe very close to the apartment where I lived at the time, I was able to stay very close. At one point, Roy was taking one hundred to two hundred and fifty pills per day. I spent many hours making sure he took them according to directions, whether it was to be on an empty stomach or with food. Also, I monitored which pills had to be taken in the morning, afternoon, or evening.

Joe relieved me at the end of each day when he returned home from work. Then two months later, and without any warning at all, Joe died. We discovered that he had been living in shame and secrecy all along. He wore diapers to work. He purchased smaller-sized clothing, so his dramatic weight loss wasn't apparent. He hid the ever-increasing sores with makeup. Lastly, he wore long sleeved shirts in the middle of the summer, a pattern very familiar to those of us surviving at the time.

Naturally, I remained Roy's primary caretaker after Joe's unexpected death. And I was beside Roy when he died a year later. Roy's death was the most devastating thing I had ever experienced. When I knew he was passing, I held him close until the warmth had moved from his body, and his limbs entered rigor mortis. Roy was my pal, and we did everything together during the decade and a half we were in a relationship. He was the person I started the journey with, and though I'd selfishly hoped that I would go first so it wouldn't be so hard, that was not to be. Roy and Joe were the last two people I had left, and when Roy passed, I fell apart.

As I waited for the coroner to arrive, I found myself reverting to a childhood behavior I had long forgotten about. I found refuge in crawling under Roy's bed and hiding there. Upon hearing my moans of distress, the coroner gently coaxed me from under the bed, where I watched Roy's body being put into a bag, zipped up tight, and wheeled away on a stretcher.

I remained in bed for three weeks after Roy's death. The sorrow was overwhelming, and it prevented me from functioning. Allowing myself the experience of feeling the feelings of such a tremendous loss was the first time I had allowed myself to feel anything since the death of my good friend Billy 15 years earlier. Each day my therapist called me and asked me to perform one task until I could eventually function on my own. This period lasted for more than six weeks.

For me, everything changed after Roy's death. I was quite numb to everything around me. I wasn't interested in my gym. I didn't want to date. I didn't want to eat. I didn't even want to socialize. My healing was slow because I couldn't rush through the tragedies I had been living with for so long. People were still dying around me, although not in the enormous numbers as before. Word spread quickly throughout our community when friends would disappear from the public eye, leaving us to learn that they were in fact deceased.

Eventually, I began to pull myself together after a process that took me at least four to five months. Little by little, I found distraction in doing more exercise videos for celebrities and fitness products. Just as I was starting to feel like myself again, I learned that my therapist had received his Ph.D. and had taken a job in Canada. We mutually decided to terminate our relationship with the knowledge that there were more areas in my life I still needed to explore. The first and most important was my HIV status and learning to confide in people that I loved and trusted. Also, I knew I needed to learn to be ready to answer and accept everything that goes with full disclosure including both of our emotions, the shock value on others, questions, medications, and the thought of dying.

CHAPTER 16

I eventually closed my gym and returned to training private clients in their homes. Inside, however, I was merely waiting to die. After all, I'd lost all of my friends, so it was easy to assume that death would come soon for me too. But as time marched on, I wondered why I was the only one left? Why hadn't I perished along with everyone else I had known and loved? By this time I had lost over a thousand people I had known. AIDS had genuinely decimated my community.

It wasn't long after that realization that I started to feel my body slowing down. Being in the health profession, I was the first to notice my decline. It was incredibly hard to hide as I was a trainer and teaching group exercise. I struggled to continue to teach up to five high impact classes per day, but then I'd return home feeling wholly and utterly exhausted. As maintaining excellent health had long meant the world me, perhaps that had been a significant factor in prolonging my life. But then again, even my healthiest friends had passed from AIDS. I then wondered if maybe it just wasn't my time. Perhaps there was more for me to do on earth?

Exercise had always been my number one survival tool. Since the time in my early youth when I ran the driveway of Frank and Martha's farmhouse, exercise had been my only outlet whenever I faced challenges throughout my life. Exercise was the one constant for me. It had always been there for me to avail myself of anything I needed to navigate, and now the one thing I could rely upon was failing me. I felt very alone and terrified as I contemplated the loss of my one survival tool. I was in a situation that appeared to have no way out, and my usual compartmental tool was no longer working.

I had been HIV positive for twenty years at that point. I hadn't taken a single drug and had vowed never to do so. I'd become afraid to make friends with gay men, so once my mostly straight friends started noticing changes in my behavior, I knew I had to act. I was increasingly sluggish, which was a far cry from the boundless energy I once had. I often lost my train of thought. I was sleeping all the time. My loss of appetite resulted in a noticeable weight loss, so I knew I needed to disclose my status.

Disclosure was not easy for me to do. Since none of my friends expected it, my biggest fear of mass panic and non-stop crying would inevitably occur, and all of my fearful thoughts and feelings became a reality once I disclosed. After the initial shock had passed for them, my friends decided to stage an intervention with the hope to convince me to start taking medication. It took a lot to convince me to do so after my experience watching beloved friends pass from the medical side effects of the powerful drugs in the earlier years.

Now the campaign to consider more than just my own feelings had a tremendous impact on me. My friends expressed their opinions in saying that my behavior was very selfish in choosing to die without exploring the advancements made in more recent years. They said refusing to at least try to take medication was unacceptable. And so it was at their urging that I reluctantly agreed to take meds.

My body was rapidly failing. I was extremely tired and overwhelmed by a general overall feeling of slowing down. I was subject to crying spells that overtook me without rhyme nor reason. A constant ear infection, sore throat, and clogged nose plagued me without end. With all the symptoms of my body slowing down, I was lucky that I didn't contract any other virus that would have escalated the HIV in my body. I was so terrified of what had become a real and looming potential outcome, that I hastily convinced and demanded that my physician prescribe as minimal a pill regime as possible. I was adamant to the point that I started with a dosage (although only one pill) that was monstrously too strong. And, as if that wasn't enough fear-based decision making, I went home, and I took it alone.

The result of its strength on my newly medicated body was overwhelming. I had crazy hallucinations. My artwork started speaking to me. I became hysterical as I watched dancers swirl about me, taunting fantastical promises of death and dying. I cried, screamed, and struggled with the reality that this was what I had to come to terms with as a new way of life. I drove to San Francisco to see a dear friend for some much-needed support. Still under the influence of the drug, I got lost in Fresno for 17 hours. Frustrated and defeated, I parked in a field, not knowing where I was or how to get back home. Hours later, and at the point where I was ready to call it in, I finally made it home and realized that was not the way I wanted to live.

When I spoke to my doctor, he apologetically convinced me to try one more prescription with the agreement that if it failed, I could walk into the sunset with his blessing. Well, it worked, and within months I felt remarkably better. I actually had no idea of just how bad of a condition I had been in. My denial had masked not only my perception of my health but also my desire to live. Once I was feeling better, I sought out another therapist to help me understand and cope with the next significant chapter in my life.

With the advancements in medical science, the virus in many of us is undetectable. I believe that during my lifetime, I will live to see a vaccine to eradicate the virus, a remarkable achievement and a great tribute to those who have gone before us. It's hard to believe that I am one of the very few still here nearly forty years after transmission. I feel that there is a reason for my survival and have chosen to believe that it's for me to share my story — to help as many people as I can make healthier choices for themselves. Whatever it may be, there is not a day that goes by that I am not sincerely grateful for who I am today. No more hiding, keeping secrets, living in fear, or controlling what people think of me.

CHAPTER 17

Being raised in the Pentecostal church ultimately resulted in my feeling a lot of guilt yet little confusion about my sexuality. For many, many years I was engaged in a constant internal struggle between what was right and what was wrong. Whenever I found a man attractive or had sexy thoughts about him, I internally branded myself a "sinner" as I had been taught that just the fact that I liked guys meant that I was doomed. There were times when I wanted to shop at an adult bookstore to buy a funny or sexy card or go to a bar to meet someone, and I would be terrified that some alarm would go off and I would be arrested. Even something as minor as saying a bad word — aloud or in my head — would incite an internal wave of sheer panic. The church sermons I'd been subjected to as a child rang on autoplay in my head. I felt eternal shame that I was doing wrong and headed straight to Hell: the scariest place you could imagine where you would burn for eternity.

Terribly frightening stories about sin were relayed to me as a kid, and I carried these constant reminders with me through college and into my adult life. I didn't fully grasp the magnitude of what I was carrying around with me until I started therapy. Only once I began addressing my earlier "programming" was I able to purposely go into places that I had considered scary or unclean and no "alarm" would go off. I came to understand what the sermons were and how they were meant to instill fear, shame, and embarrassment in the congregation. As an adult I learned that all the stories, parables, and sermons told to me as a kid were not my reality: they were someone else's manipulation designed to instill fear and force me to behave a certain way.

Therapy guided me to become the person I am today. My first therapist, Dr. Sean, helped me hone the essential tools to take care of myself and take responsibility for my actions. With Dr. Sean, I learned how to express my fears and bring them to a healthier place. I could go into areas that once represented everything the Bible and sermons of the past demoralized, and that had previously sent me to the dark side. I could enter these places without spiraling into shame, remorse, and self-disgust. Instead, I could feel just fine and actually enjoy myself around other men who were like me. I learned how I compartmentalized, and with Dr. Sean's help, I integrated all my disparate parts into a whole person functioning together all of the time. I learned to understand my feelings and communicate them freely without fear of how I would be received.

Therapy gave me the courage to petition the court to have the records of my life as a foster child unsealed. It enabled me to return to Ohio and find my birth parents, Lenore and Paul, as well as initiate my process of forgiveness and closure with the two of them. Many years later, I felt blessed to be at their sides when they took their final breaths. Even today, therapy continues to help me explore areas of my life that saddened me, strengthened me, destroyed me, and empowered me. This introspection continues to be a crucial part of my survival.

Like most any other child with a God-given right to exist, all I had ever wanted was to give love and to receive love. Before entering therapy, I only knew how to offer as I didn't understand, nor was I taught, the boundaries of healthy, reciprocal love. I gave so much of myself to others that I would be utterly unbalanced and ultimately depleted. I would get sick, yet never feel confident enough to show it or complain for fear of being moved to another foster home. The constant feeling or the threat of being moved stayed with me well into my adulthood even though I was never physically moved. These feelings also showed up as a fear of being abandoned or not liked. In the earlier days of my adulthood, I created a crazy kind of point system in my head. If I did more and gave more to the guy I was dating, then I would be safe, and he wouldn't leave me. This made some kind of sense to me at that time, as I wanted to avoid feeling hurt or rejected. As much as I tried to "give" with loads of presents and affection, my point system always failed. Without a healthy understanding of boundaries and reciprocal love, I went out of my way to let anyone take advantage of me, just to feel wanted for however long it would last. My earlier self had zero self-worth.

It took me many years in therapy to work through my trauma, patterns, and history to learn about myself — seventeen years, to be exact. To this day, I still check in with my therapist to make sure I'm on track. It's a continual process for me. At first, everything was so foreign to me, and much of my progress had to be based on learning to trust another human being. While I felt ready to change, there were times when I felt stuck with a thought or behavior without knowing how to break through. I relied on patience and the knowing that I had a history of breakthroughs made it easier for me to work harder. Once I discovered that my lack of self-worth was the core root of my troubles, I had to learn to use the word "no" without giving in to the fear of being disliked.

As a foster child, survival had been the only goal I had ever known how to set, so receiving love was the carrot that dangled in front of me at the end of every path I ran — metaphorical or literal. At first as an adult, setting boundaries felt like an impossible task. Would people like me if I set a limit? What if I said no? Or if I refused to give more of myself than was healthy for me? It was a brave new world as I set out on this journey as an adult in my forties. Therapy gave me permission and taught me to love myself, which was the hardest and most foreign step for me in the beginning. With a lot of trial and error, I experimented with people I trusted and found the power of self-love.

Once I had left Frank and Martha's home for college, I was on my own in every sense of the word. I had to learn everything — from how to manage money, pay bills, file taxes, make rent, and ensure I had enough money left over to purchase food — while also navigating through the world with my head held high. Therapy helped me understand how to reshape and learn all of those tasks so I could comprehend how to become a more successful and stable person inside and out. I learned how to find balance without compromising myself. The more change I saw in myself, the more I wanted to learn; and as I changed, everything around me began to change as well. People treated me differently, and I created a whole new set of friends. I was able to minimize the "takers" in my life and build more healthy balanced relationships. What I learned most profoundly was that I was always the hardest on myself.

Whether I learned or I was taught, from a very young age I believed that my actions, feelings, and emotions were wrong. I am still to this day finding areas within myself to forgive. It's tough work to go inside and see the places that I shut down, acknowledge them, love them, and let them go. Shame was one of the most significant areas I had to address. I felt shame for choices I had made, shame around where I came from, shame for who I loved, and shame for the lengths I would go to have even five to ten minutes of acknowledgment. But, for any of that healing and those changes to take place for me, I first had to forgive others — a process that will never end. I always strive for the best for me as well as for those around me.

While loving myself was one of my most challenging processes, today I am much closer than I have ever been. I know that because in recent years I met someone who shows me love in a way I had never experienced before. He is kind, generous, and he understands who he is and where he's going. He holds me in a space that is the safest I've ever known. It has taken me a while to adjust and accept that this is what love really feels and looks like. And I now understand that I am so blessed to finally be in a place to explore, give, and rejoice in love and happiness. I owe a lot of this newfound wisdom and joy to all the work I've done and to the people who created a safe place for me to grow. I appreciate all the people who loved me and stood by me through the times when I was at my lowest points. I now know how to make real friendships, and consider myself fortunate that I have four or five solid friends that I know I can call at any time and they will be there for me with no questions or judgments. To me, that is one of the greatest gifts a person can have.

Therapy has gifted me with amazing coping skills. Now I look at situations differently and quickly adapt to things that are out of my control. Instead of running away with fear or avoiding the situation entirely, I deal with those things that seem at first to be overwhelming. I know how to take the situation apart and look at the parts I know I can handle and start to work from there. Panic is not my go-to emotion anymore. I understand that although I was dealt a series of cards for my life, it is my choice in how I play them. My choices enable me to move forward to be the best person I can be. Looking back at my struggles, I see how sometimes I messily persevered. It was Dr. Sean and Dr. William who guided and believed in me. In their different ways, they helped me to rise above and see what I thought was impossible to overcome. They were the eyes that I trusted when I couldn't see. They held me up to run forward when I didn't believe I could even stand. They will forever be sources of inspiration and guidance in my heart.

CHAPTER 18

Frank Kidd was the first of my four parental figures to die. His work in the coal mines as a young man, combined with his lifelong love for tobacco, caused the development of black lung which eventually developed into lung cancer. Frank rolled a beautiful cigarette like most men from his era — a prideful display that defined his generation. During his final days in the hospital, I flew from my home in California to visit him, bringing a little whistle to make him laugh. The day he passed, barely able to speak, he motioned for me to come close. While I held his hand, he gently whispered, "I'm sorry for not being a better father. I should have thrown a baseball, and come to watch you wrestle or compete in track and field." I assured him that I felt he was the best father I could have asked for. I thanked him for his love. For men of his generation, supporting a son through athletics was their only way to show emotion.

Ten years after Frank's death, I finally convinced Martha to visit me in Los Angeles. It was the most magical time I had ever spent with Martha as she saw the ocean for the first time. Having never stood on a beach or understanding the motion of the ocean, she giggled in delight as the tides rolled in and out to caress her bare feet.

Disneyland was equally as entertaining for both her and for me to witness. She insisted on purchasing a souvenir book to capture every character autograph from Cinderella to Cruella Deville. We stayed until midnight when the park closed. Having had those experiences so often myself, I had taken them for granted. To watch the childlike excitement of a 70-year-old woman was really something to behold. The tables had magically shifted in our relationship.

During her visit to California, Martha shared with me that she didn't have much time left, and asked me to be her caretaker. In an interesting reversal of life, I flew back to Ohio to care for her during her final three months. In that time, Martha was able to say goodbye to many of the children she had fostered during her 35 years as a foster mother. Although I was with her when she died in her sleep, I did not receive my final goodbye from her. I'm not sure what that would have looked or felt like, but I took comfort knowing that she died peacefully and safely.

Without hesitation, I graciously accepted the invitation from the family to perform her eulogy. Inspired by a children's book I'd read months earlier entitled *A Mother for Choco*, I crafted my speech. The core message of the book expressed the importance of family love no matter how different parents and children may be, and whether birthed, fostered, or adopted. Choco, a small yellow bird, wished for a mother, but who could she be? He sets off to find her, asking different animals for advice, but he doesn't meet anyone who looks like him. He discovers physical traits that are like him in the penguin and walrus, but to his dismay, they don't want him. It's clear to him not to ask Mrs. Bear, but to his surprise, she starts to do just the things a mommy might do. She asks, "If you had a mommy, what would she do?"

Choco replies that she would hug him.

"Well, I can hug you, what else?" Mrs. Bear asks.

"She would kiss me goodnight and sing me a lullaby," Choco says.

"Well, I can do that, too," Mrs. Bear replies.

"Will you dance with me and cheer me up?" Chico asks.

"I would be delighted to do so," Mrs. Bear says with a loving embrace. She invites him home where he meets her children. He's shocked and amazed by what he sees: a piglet, a hippo, and an alligator among many other different types of animals. He comes to understand that families can come in all shapes and sizes and still fit together.

This was the message I found to describe best the courageous woman who spent her life giving to children in need. As I spoke, my emotions were all over the place. Every feeling seemed to be attached to an event or time in my life with Martha Kidd. Even as this was taking place inside, I was surrounded by calmness outside. I spoke gently and with compassion, lifting her image and love to the highest place possible. I knew this was where our journey together would end on this plane, however, I was still striving to be that perfect little boy.

Once the funeral was over and Martha's affairs were in order, it was time to return home. At the airport ticket counter, the agent noticed my puffy eyes and congestion and inquired about my sad demeanor. I explained my situation. With tears in her eyes, the agent shared that her mother had just passed as well and it was her first day back to work. As she was processing the ticket, the agent noted that her mother had the last name as mine. Our chance meeting indicated to us that something more significant in the universe wanted us to meet. Through our shared experience and tearful exchange, she handed me a first-class ticket to Los Angeles. I looked up, thanking Martha for her *bon voyage* and the sweet kiss on my cheek. I realized right then that she was still with me, watching over me, and she always would be.

Thank you, Mom.

CHAPTER 19

When I was in my thirties, and after much consideration, I petitioned to have my records unsealed. After making significant progress in therapy, I had reached the point where I wanted to learn about my early life and my relatives. This was quite a process in which I wrote a letter to the Medina courthouse to request the records from the time I entered foster care until I aged out. Several months later, I received notice that my records were released, and I was given a court-appointed time frame within which to complete my goal. I booked a flight back to Ohio with great anticipation of what I was going to learn.

When I arrived at the courthouse, I was ushered into a tiny closet-like room with a small desk, a chair, and a second chair for the security guard. The walls were painted a pale shade, and most of the floor tiles had been peeled away. The smell in the room was that of old papers being kept in a storage room: musty and damp. The ominous tower of stacked files that greeted me went from the floor to the ceiling. I was instructed not to take pictures, notes or make copies of anything provided for me. I had only my memory on which to remember the details of what I read. Knowing the court would allow me one eight-hour day to read these files, I took a deep breath and picked up the first file folder.

I spent the next eight hours reading about my life, only stopping to catch the breath frozen in my throat, or to wipe the stream of tears that ran from my eyes. Of course, there were no computers back then, so every line and entry was either handwritten or typed and to my surprise, most entries were quite neat and organized. Through the eyes of the many social workers in charge of my case, I was introduced to every previously unrevealed aspect of my young life. I learned about the times and places that had significantly affected the course of my life, starting with the painful descriptions of the state I was in when I was initially found in that crib in Lenore's apartment. I read about my early emotional struggles when I was first put into foster care and the state of my mental health, including the descriptions of my uncontrollable moments of deep despair and how I cried for hours after Lenore would visit. Those visits were stopped after the court deemed that it was psychologically damaging for her to visit me.

Some of the files were thick with evidence from everything from medical visits to school vaccinations to observances about my mental health. Dental reports indicated that I had teeth pulled because of an abscess that had developed. The reports contained notations that I was not receiving proper care from doctors, and on one occasion when I did visit a doctor for a bug bite, I was given too much penicillin and passed out. I read about the physical abuse that was presented as punishment at Mrs. Smith's when I didn't use the right utensil or say please or thank you in foster care. It was noted that I was always asking what was going to happen to me. The process of receiving clothing a mere three times a year was detailed, as well as the fact that I had to start work as a janitor at the age of ten to pay for my clothes when the foster care clothing allowance was discontinued.

I learned that Lenore and Paul had divorced in 1959 and within months of their split, Lenore met Bob, a local fireman. She spent the rest of her life with Bob, and they were married for well over forty years until Lenore passed at the age of seventy. My birth father, Paul, had already been seeing a nurse named Carol for some time when he married her. They had a child together, but tragedy soon struck Paul's new family. Carol died six months later after going blind and receiving a double amputation due to undetected diabetes. Their infant daughter, Yvonne, was put in foster care. My half-sister, unfortunately, developed the same condition as her mother and died at a very young age. We met several times, but her illness was so advanced by that point that there wasn't much time or opportunity for us to connect. Paul never married again, choosing to live out the rest of his days with his sister. The details about my father are sparse. I know he worked for a mattress company and was a member of the local Rotary Club.

I did make it a point to find the name of the social worker in my files who made it possible for me to go to college. I filed her name away in that sacred part of my brain as I did not want to forget that unsung angel from my past. After several months, I found her by email and was able to express my gratitude to her about how she had helped create opportunities for me that otherwise wouldn't have come my way. She responded by telling me that she had been a social worker for only a single year, and

I felt fortunate that I had come under her purview during that time. She went on to have eight other careers before settling down to raise her family. It was great to hear from her, and we stayed in contact for several years before our communication came to a natural end.

When I left the courthouse that evening, despite feeling mentally, physically, and emotionally exhausted, I experienced a tremendous sense of empowerment in having so many questions answered that had been with me for much of my life. It was a life-changing and very powerful day. In many ways, it was a blessing that I read my records before meeting my relatives in the following years. I had read in my files about how many times Lenore and Paul had been approached to sign papers to let us be adopted. Each time the pair was contacted, the requests to sever the birth relationships had been denied. Had I read the records before our meeting, I would likely have been much more confrontational and angry with their choices and what I learned to understand was neglect. It would have been an entirely different meeting than the one I experienced. Looking back, I see that things always are precisely the way they are supposed to be.

CHAPTER 20

Although I learned where Paul lived, I waited to contact him for several years. I'm not entirely sure why I waited to look him up, but the possibility of being rejected on some level loomed large in the back of my mind. Also, I knew I needed time to work on myself, and so I initially had no intention of ever reaching out to Paul and Lenore but entering therapy was the catalyst that motivated me to seek them out. I was aware that Paul would know where to find Lenore. I also knew my window of opportunity was limited because neither one of them would be expecting a visit from me. With so many things to ask and to tell, I hoped to make a solid connection with my real parents. On some level, I guess I was looking for approval from them when I made that journey back to Ohio. I was anxious and ready when I started my journey, as I had a lot to say and wasn't sure how much time I had, how well I would be received, or what their reactions would be to the things I wanted to share. I had so many thoughts, but the most pressing was that I hoped to hear that they loved each other when I was born.

When Paul and I met, the realization that my actual father was next to me was overwhelming. I was deeply moved to be near him. I lacked a real understanding of father-son bonding and was deeply curious about what this looked like. I had one simple question: what did my father look like naked? This question is not as absurd as you might think, and my therapist had assured me that mine was a very reasonable question. Most kids get to see their parents naked when they are young. As an adult, most of my friends talked about their inadvertent and accidental viewings of their naked parents during childhood. After having been raised by another man with whom I shared no genetics, I wanted to know if my father and I shared similar physical traits. As we drove to Lenore's house, I decided to ask Paul if I could see him naked. He looked at me with a gentle, fatherly smile and replied, "Anytime you want." As soon as he said that, the question went away.

Lenore was quite surprised (to put it mildly) to find Paul and me on her doorstep, inviting her to spend time with us. She was the epitome of what I had imagined. Lenore wore very tightly rolled curls combed into the most modest hairstyle of the time, and wore a flowered high-waisted dress covered with a full apron. She was also quite round for someone who was only 4'8" in stature. I saw that I had her hair color and her blue eyes and that I shared Paul's strong chin and body shape. For just a slight moment, I felt complete. We then proceeded to have a somewhat awkward lunch together at a nearby (and possibly the closest) diner. Sitting in front of the two of them for the first time was quite surreal. I took a moment to savor the experience of knowing that these people were my real parents — that, together, they had me. Oddly, they ordered the exact same thing I ordered for lunch: a chicken sandwich, coleslaw, and french fries. We ate in strained silence.

Knowing that I would be nervous, I had prepared an outline for everything I wanted to say to them. On my lap, I had one paper for Paul, one for Lenore, and then one for both of them. I started with both of them. The first item on the outline I addressed was, "I want you to know that I'm gay." To this disclosure, I was met with a blank reaction. Neither one of them displayed a single emotion. It seemed as if maybe they had known all along that I was gay, but most of the information I gave them elicited little to no reaction. For the duration of the lunch, they both appeared to be trying to process the moments. I found myself reiterating over and over again to them that the meeting was about me and my journey to find closure. I soon knew this would be the first and last time I would see them both together, as their hostility for each other became apparent. I was shocked to learn that our lunch was the first time they had seen each other since my sister, brother, and I were taken away from Lenore thirty-four years earlier. With all the courage I could muster, I reminded them again that this meeting was for me. My biggest question for them was whether or not they had been in love with each other when I was conceived. Already knowing that they likely were not, I thought to myself that if they weren't, I hoped they would only let me believe that they were. I was happy that they did so.

I ended our lunch date by inviting them to stay in touch with me. As I paid the bill, there was no offer from either one to cover the check or assist in any way. After lunch, I gave them each one hundred dollars to buy a new cell phone with the hope that they would check in with me at least once a month. I did my best to try to get a commitment from each of them. Paul was initially receptive. He did purchase a phone, but then he rarely called.

On the other hand, Lenore admitted that she spent the money on something other than a phone. She then proceeded to write nasty letters in which she accused me of disrupting her life. Lenore wrote that I was never her favorite child, and would never be. I caused her to remember things she merely wanted to forget. She called me terrible names and continuously asked me for money because she'd brought me into this world.

For years I received these missives from Lenore, which tore me apart. Eventually, I just stopped reading her letters and pretended they didn't exist. I already knew I wasn't her favorite, as she always made that clear when as a child she'd brought me hand-me-down clothes that were too small, broken toys that didn't work, and cards that had been sent to her on which she'd struck a line through the original name and added mine. Throughout this entire time and despite how mean she was, I was never able to let go of the hope that one day Lenore would find it within herself to love me. I continued to visit her whenever I traveled to Ohio, but during my visits, she would only ask about my sister and not me, which eventually became very frustrating. Finally, I said that they only lived an hour away from each other and could reach out to her daughter at any time. She never did reach out, and so she was unable to meet her daughter or her grandchildren until right before her death.

Inexplicably, Lenore blamed me for her pain, as well as for the results of most of the choices she had made in her life. She did this because she knew that no matter how poorly she treated me, I would always be there for her.

Somehow, this was acceptable to me. There were several times I reached out and sent her money because I just wanted to make sure she was okay. She felt as though I owed her for bringing me into this world and she would always remind me of such. Once the money was sent, I never heard whether she received it or not. There were no thankyous. Not ever.

My sister and I are very close to this day. As we shared the experience of being moved from Lenore, we always knew we were fortunate to have been placed in our two foster homes together. Most kids get separated from their siblings when they enter the foster care system. My sister has a different perspective, being she is two years older than me. Despite being the younger sibling, I always felt as though I needed to protect her, but she was always smarter than I was in school and achieved considerable recognition. She got married right out of high school as many girls do who exit foster care. Her first marriage lasted eight years before they divorced. She married again, had two amazing kids, and now works as a gemologist. Unlike me, she did not have the desire to see her records or to know anything about Lenore or Paul.

CHAPTER 21

When I was thirty-five years old, Lenore's mother, my grandmother, died. My sister and I made the decision to attend her funeral, which was the first time we were able to meet our aunts and uncles on both sides. For forty years, not one member of our extended family had made a single effort to reach out to us. This was so confusing, as at any given time any one of them could have removed us from foster care. They could have adopted one or all of us, yet they remained utterly silent. When my sister and I met these many aunts and uncles and were able to ask why they didn't take us out of foster care, the general reply was that three kids were too much. We believed that instead, it was about the shameful, incestuous family secret. I don't have much information about the many aunts and uncles, other than one was a professional tennis player, and many of Lenore's aunts love to quilt. Most of the men on Paul's side enjoyed hunting and fishing, and I had nothing in common with many of them.

My brother Jimmy had moved into his own place when he was eighteen years old. Within two years, he started to rapidly decline both mentally and physically, so Martha took him into the house so together we could care for him. It was quite a struggle to move, clean, and feed him on a daily basis as he continued to decline. Jimmy lost all of his adult functions, his fine and gross motor skills, and the ability to think clearly and express his needs. Within weeks he started to display the behaviors of an infant. He could no longer feed himself, so he had to be bottle-fed, and placed in diapers. Jimmy could only communicate in infantile language and responded only to brightly colored toys. Martha generously cared for him until the responsibilities became overwhelming. I helped as best I could, but Martha and I realized he needed proper care. After a year of taking care of him, we decided to put him into a facility that would give him the 24-hour-a-day care that he needed at that point. Within a few months, his organs began to shut down, and Jimmy soon passed.

As I watched him decline over those years, I became worried that his specific condition existed in my family genetics. As a fifteen-year-old boy, I misunderstood in thinking that his was a hereditary condition, and became afraid the same thing was going to happen to me. I expressed my fear and asked for an autopsy to be performed on my brother. The results showed that he was actually the child of my mother and her brother: a dark secret that had been kept silent for years. Finally, the truth was discovered, and I learned why twenty-five aunts and uncles would not take us out of foster care. Their shame was so great that they chose to ostracize their sister — my mother — for her indiscretion, and that took precedence over loving us. There was never any mention of Jim's dad, who was our uncle. At the time, the blame always fell on the girl, and my uncle took no responsibility for his actions, either physically or financially.

Although we had intermittently stayed in touch, my relationship with Paul was somewhat strained. This was mostly since he didn't approve of me being gay. I didn't blame him. I felt it was his level of ignorance, combined with a very redneck short-sighted upbringing, that resulted in his feeling this way. However, I did my best to involve him in my life. At an earlier time, I wanted to introduce him to someone I was seeing. I arranged a meeting for the three of us to meet at Paul's house, yet after hours of waiting, he never showed. Feeling broken-hearted and confused, my boyfriend and I left Ohio. I vowed never to return. My boyfriend at the time had a lot of discord at his home, and he was very supportive, while I was furious. That's when it became clear to me that Paul avoided anything and everything that had to do with my sexual orientation. The incident of him not showing up was like a pitchfork through my heart.

During the final days when I was taking care of my adoptive mother, Martha, Paul called to tell me he had been given only six months to live. It was a very trying time for me. After Martha passed and I was able to collect myself, I flew back to Ohio to visit Paul. My duty to honor my parents as spoken from the Bible propelled me to ask Paul during my visit, "As your only son, is there anything I could do for you to make your last days comfortable?" His reply was no. I told him that the visit was going to be my last, and thanked him for bringing me into the world. I totally understand now that my presence in this situation was a constant reminder of his failure. Yet, like Lenore, he also knew that I would be there in the end.

Two months later, I was vacationing on the East Coast when my sister called to say that Paul's health was failing but he refused to die until I got there. Begrudgingly, I flew back to Ohio. I went to his house and realized that his daily care had become too much for his sister. One of the main struggles she was having was in bathing him, so she asked if I would do so. As I gently washed him, it occurred to me that I was finally seeing my father naked for the first time. It indeed was a father-son bonding moment for me. I once again thanked him for bringing me into this world as I dressed him in his pajamas. Once in bed, he waited no more than fifteen minutes before drifting away, silently and peacefully. At his funeral, a small group of people assembled to celebrate his life including his Rotary friends. As I introduced myself to them, thanking them for being in his life, I was saddened but not surprised to learn that not a single one of them — his close friends of thirty years or more — had known that Paul had a son.

Years later, I received word from Lenore's stepdaughter that Lenore had suffered a stroke. I immediately flew back to Ohio and drove ninety miles in a blizzard to reach Lenore's home where I found her and her husband Bob, whom I had never met, in a tiny, rundown, dilapidated old house. Since the majority of the ceiling had caved in from the snow, Lenore and Bob lived in the one room that had a ceiling structure, and who knew how long that would have lasted. Blankets covered the walls, and the only heat came from a tiny electric heater.

Lenore's physical condition wasn't much better than her surroundings as her entire left side was paralyzed and she was incontinent. The bathroom had been buried by snow weeks before my arrival. The smell emanating from the bucket she was using for a toilet permeated the entire space to such a degree I could barely breathe. I was horrified by their living conditions and soon became emotionally distraught. So many emotions washed over me and I was unable to think clearly. I did not want them to witness my utter despair, so I redirected my energy and visualized how to get them out of there. I stayed an extra week to find a low-income housing apartment with a medical facility attached. I moved them in, helped them get settled, and set up regular doctor and nursing visits. Feeling that they were safe and would be taken care of, I returned to my home in Los Angeles. One month later, I received a phone call from the facility: Lenore and Bob had moved out and returned to their single room dwelling.

A month later, I received a call from the same stepdaughter saying Lenore had less than a week to live. I took the red-eye back to Ohio. I managed to convince my sister to visit and allow Lenore to meet her grandchildren for the first time. An hour after my sister, her husband, their two kids and I left the hospital, Lenore had a heart attack that left her in a coma. Two days later, she died with my sister and me in the room.

Bob asked me to go with him to the funeral home to make arrangements. His insistence that I help make the decisions on the details of Lenore's burial made me feel for the first time a closeness to Lenore that I had never experienced before. Once the arrangements were finalized, and payment was due, Bob confessed that there was no money. He informed me that Lenore had said to him, "Don't worry. Tim will take care of it all." I took all of my savings out and buried her. I felt manipulated and used and had to work very hard not to be bitter towards her.

I have complete closure with all four of my parental figures in my life. It has been a real blessing to have been with each of them as they departed this earth for the next realm of light. I love them. I forgive them. I thank them. And I celebrate the choices they made. Those choices have shaped me into the person I've become today.

CHAPTER 22

When I had moved to Los Angeles to pursue a career in fitness, I landed my first of many high-profile clients that included CEOs of movie studios, actresses, actors, singers, and band members. Some were just starting out, and others would later become incredibly famous, while others were legends in their own right. I traveled with them on tour and trained them before their performances at night. One of them had been acting since she was in her teens and had become a household name. When she invited me to go on a field trip to a children's home, I was excited to oblige her.

Soon the day arrived when I stepped foot on a charter bus full of "A-list" Hollywood power-hitter activists. There wasn't a single woman on that bus that I hadn't seen at least a dozen times on the silver screen. Most of these women were committed to this work every week, and I was thrilled to join them, as I shared the very same passion for helping children. Even though they were decked out in Gucci, Chanel, and Prada, and dripping with wealth, they were kind and generous women who genuinely wanted to make a difference. Most of them had kids of their own who were grown, yet they treated each child at the home as if they were their own. After meeting and enjoying their company, many of the ladies eventually became clients of mine.

The initial event my client invited me to was called Perfect Personal Hygiene Day, which was held at a children's home in El Monte, California. This particular activity was conducted twice a month, with the primary goal to teach the children how to properly navigate personal hygiene. We brought gifts and clothes for the children because the donations for this organization were off-the-charts generous. There was always plenty of food and live music, as well as outrageous and challenging games that were often led by sports celebrities.

After several visits with the ladies to the home, I noticed that there wasn't any place available for the kids to exercise and dance. Knowing I had the resources to create a space that could serve that need, I raised enough money to build a gym on the premises. The total project cost was fifty thousand dollars, and I was able to raise the entire amount through private donations. I knew that unless the staff was excited about the project, then the kids wouldn't be either, so I drove to the children's home twice a week for a solid year to train the staff. Most of the crew ate poorly and were very overweight, so I taught them how to exercise, eat right, and take care of themselves. Over the year, most of them lost weight, increased their cardio, learned how to lift weights, and how to get their bodies moving. By the time the gym was finished, the staff was ready, excited, and motivated to help the kids. I then created affiliations with nearby gyms to enable different instructors to teach dance, yoga, and many other classes at the children's home.

Up to that point, my relationship with women had been at best, unstable. First abandoned, then relocated into foster care, and finally placed under the jurisdiction of forty-four female social workers left me feeling distrustful toward women, to say the least. Through therapy, I learned that it was from those experiences and the lack of bonding with women that made me continually strive to be the perfect boy. In pursuit of that perfection, I knew and anticipated everything in my environment that would make me feel safe. My observation was an art form, and I had the "perfect boy" act down cold.

My efforts at the children's home were quite successful, and I was soon recognized by the founder of the organization, Lisa McCoy. She was everything I imagined a woman should be: beautiful, smart, athletic, and, most of all, driven. She was petite in stature at 5'2" and 105 pounds, which made her the envy of most women in that she could wear anything and look amazing. She was very obsessed with how she looked and the way she presented herself. As a true disciple of beauty enhancements, she was always up on the latest trend, in great shape with toned arms, legs, and body. She knew she had a great body and would use it to her benefit if necessary.

Lisa thanked me for all I had done for the children's home and in speaking with me expressed the desire to work with a personal trainer for aerobics. She hired me on the spot that day, and I soon advanced to be her full-time trainer. I went to her house every Tuesday, Thursday, and Saturday morning at 7:30, a practice that would continue for the next thirty years.

CHAPTER 23

Lisa became everything to me as I trained her for the next three decades. Throughout our time together she became a mother, sister, best friend, and confidant to me. As a result of her working with foster kids for many years, Lisa understood every nuance of a foster child's needs. Consequently, as I discovered years later, she calculatingly gave me every material item I didn't have as a child, as well as the loving qualities I so desperately longed for while growing up. I believe to this day that Lisa loved me as much as she was capable of loving another person. After all, I worked overtime to make her smile and laugh. I would tell her stories while she was on the treadmill to pass the time. Seeing her happy was magical to me.

During our friendship, I came to learn why she had abruptly fired her weight trainer. It was discovered that she was having an affair with him over several months, which marked her first divorce from her husband of thirty years. As fate would have it, I conveniently stepped into the role of trainer and confidante. She confided more than I wanted to know, and I soon found myself wishing I didn't know quite so much. However, on the other hand, that was the first time in my young adult life I honestly felt needed and empowered. I had the key: I knew I could influence the course of her day by merely being there for her. That is what hooked me into the long, arduous, often painful, degrading, and humiliating relationship we developed over the years. But, in spite of that, with my toolbox of coping skills, I could compartmentalize all those details as our relationship grew stronger and I gained more information. Lisa was one of the first real Hollywood wives, and I placed her on a pedestal so high that any twirling ballerina atop a music box would envy her position.

Lisa liked to throw enormous parties that she packed with the most famous celebrities. It was amazing to see how elaborate these parties were, who would attend, the dress attire of both the men and the women, as well as enjoy the musical celebrities and the provocative entertainment. Every attendee always left with a personalized gift. To this little farm boy, it was really something quite extraordinary. In a funny twist of fate, those parties led her to receive a more substantial settlement in her first divorce proceedings. Her lawyer argued that the parties had nurtured her husband's professional transactions and that she should, therefore, get a more substantial share of his business as at the time he was the head of one of the largest movie studios. She won and was subsequently awarded hundreds of million dollars in the settlement. That was the first time I saw the side of Lisa that was tough and unwilling to back down.

Lisa struggled with her children as two of them battled heroin addictions. She remained tough and determined to win those battles too, and as per her usual, she created yet another façade that no one could see through. She always had to be perfect, well-spoken, and on the prowl to create opportunities to be more powerful. She was the first person

I told that I was HIV positive. I went to her first because at the time because I was the closest to her at the time. I also was getting colds and sinus infections on a regular basis. She told me that she cried in private for a while and then decided to go into action to create a family of support for me. It was the first time I felt supported, but I came to realize the "support family" was in place to stage an intervention to convince me to take medication. Even though it was at first unsuccessful, I waited several years and then did start on a successful regime.

Once Lisa became officially single, I became a more prominent part of her life, and this kicked me into high gear. I anticipated her wants and expectations and met them before she even realized her need. Within months, I took on more and more responsibilities. I either brought or made gifts for her friends, which led to my doing all of the Christmas buying for her kids, step-children, grandchildren, and all their spouses. On holidays, I dressed as Santa Claus, the Easter Bunny, action figures, or anything that pertained to holiday excitement for the children. I started planning the birthday parties, as well as the dinner parties. I also bought and arranged all of the flowers for the different events while still working full time as a trainer at the gym.

It was a fascinating experience to be in what I called the bubble of the very rich and famous for over three decades. Lisa was a big part of the bubble, and everything she did, and the services she used were also sought out by others in the bubble. And as Lisa's trainer, I became the fitness guru. At one point I was training eight billionaires. I was one of the very few to have longevity and sustainability because most health and bodyworkers of that time were often quickly discarded for the newest flashy idea in fitness. And, as I witnessed, they were usually executed via a tart voicemail from the assistants.

Lisa became the Los Angeles version of Glenda the Good Witch, and she may as well have arrived in a pink bubble each time she showed up at an event. She met her next husband several years later by an unexpected landing on the Mayor's Mansion of Los Angeles. They would date for eight years before getting married in Sun Valley, Idaho, where she had purchased a beautiful estate. We flew there in the winters to ski. Sun Valley is one of the most prestigious and exclusive ski resort towns in the world where the insanely rich go skiing. Lisa always made sure she and I had a ski instructor at all times, and I was always on guard to make sure that she was safe. She also bought three neighboring houses in Malibu, which she promptly had torn down to build what was then the most considerable estate on Carbon Beach.

I flew privately with Lisa quite often, not only to Sun Valley but to London, Paris, Tahiti — anywhere she wanted to go. On these trips, she tended to remind me that since she was paying for everything, I should be grateful. This both humiliated and embarrassed me, but based on my past experiences with a long line of women in my life, I was able to put my feelings away and accept her generosity graciously. I loved (so I thought) this woman. I held her in such a high place that not much could blemish her in my eyes.

Therefore, I was always able to brush aside her caustic remarks or her cruel actions to remain loyal. I supported her, even though she would always remind me that I wasn't an actual part of her family. I continued to create and set up her parties, only to be asked to leave right before the guests were due to arrive. She often reminded me that it was a privilege to be with her and if I ever did something wrong, she would destroy me and I would never work in LA again. I had no doubts about her capabilities in that regard, and I frightfully watched her do that very thing to people she didn't like.

There were times I stepped a bit closer to the line by casually saying something to one of her friends I happened to be training. Although any remark of mine would indeed be harmless, after being scolded I realized Lisa worked so hard to maintain and sharpen her image, and she was not about to let anyone but me see that particular side of her. Everybody wanted to be like Lisa. She always made everything she did look so easy, and she was therefore envied by her friends. Her girlfriends dressed like her and waited to see what she would wear so they could run out and buy the same thing in a different color. During our years of friendship, we never talked about me. Our relationship was all about her and how fabulous she was.

Lisa's bubble was so masterfully constructed that she never really cared to come out of it and see how the real world operated. As long as I showed up on time, dressed to her exact specifications, and drove an acceptable car (a BMW she insisted I lease), then we were okay. She was very critical of what I wore and thought nothing of embarrassing me publicly several times when she disapproved of my choices. She gave me mixed signals, one being that I was part of the family and her closest confidant, and then two that I worked for her and she could dismiss me at will. When she would get mad at me, she would communicate through her secretary, often while I was in the very same room. Not only was I training Lisa three times a week, but I had other clients that I taught as well. She would pay me for my training yet then decide to pay what she felt like giving me for the other jobs I took on with the ever-constant reminder that I should feel fortunate to be with her at all.

I began to have a lot of difficulty in my position of trying to keep Lisa happy. In 2004, I started with my new therapist, Dr. William, to deal with taking medication and talk with him about what was going on in my life. I confessed that I would spread myself so thin to make her happy that I was becoming run down and sick. In that exploration of truth and honesty, I started taking a look at why I maintained such a toxic relationship. Slowly, I began to conjure the courage to end it. I was still in the developmental years of my burgeoning self-respect at that time, yet as I look back, I realize the absurdity of what I allowed to happen. For example, I wouldn't permit myself to use the restroom when I was with Lisa because I was afraid of making her wait. Several times she reprimanded me for the slightest delay in the schedule, regardless of whether it was my doing or hers. I never said no to her, corrected her, or suggested anything other than what I knew she wanted. Those were the things I first dared to change.

It wasn't easy. As soon as Lisa noticed that my behavior had changed, she would adapt and up her manipulation game by bringing me closer to her and making glorious yet idle promises. The central promise was repeated for years. She was going to buy me a house. I would get so excited, and on the day it was time to sign, she would change her mind. She pulled this stunt several times before I finally had enough. After her usual series of punishments, I would acquiesce to her needs only to be discarded once again. This vicious and debilitating cycle would repeat itself until one day I finally developed the nerve to tell her that we were finished.

After weeks without communication, I arrived at her home for our next agreed-upon training session. I showed up at her door ready to take action and have the big talk. I knew I had to approach our meeting as if it was business as usual, and then find the right time to tell her my feelings. I was ready to end our relationship that day, yet when I arrived at her home, I was shocked to discover a frail, depleted woman in Lisa's place. Her complexion was utterly yellow and sallow, and I knew at once that she was very ill. I rushed her to the hospital where we learned that Lisa had pancreatic cancer. After much research, as well as a generous donation, Lisa was moved to the top of the list and scheduled for major surgery a week after her diagnosis at Johns Hopkins Medical Center. That following Monday, Lisa went in for a fifteen-hour surgery and I remained with her the entire time.

CHAPTER 24

Naturally, everything I intended to do or say regarding Lisa went out the door with her terrible diagnosis. I flew with her to Baltimore, where I spent every day in the hospital with her. Everything in LA was put on hold until I was able to return, which turned out to be fifteen days later. After her surgery, I rubbed her feet and encouraged her to walk down the hall. Although I was quite exhausted, I made sure she had everything she needed. I was not only dealing with her stuff but to my own medical needs at the time as well. Luckily, I was adjusting nicely to the new therapeutic regimen I was on and could give 100% of my attention to Lisa. Yet, oddly there were times throughout her many stays in the hospital that she would remind me that if I were ever hospitalized, she would not visit me. At such confessions, I would just smile with the most profound hurt in my belly knowing she was telling the truth.

When Lisa had her pancreas removed, she was turned into a radical diabetic. I had to learn how to administer her shots and calculate her blood sugar levels. I was so in it at that point that there was no way I could leave her then. The guilt would have been unbearable. After her initial surgery, the doctor informed her that cancer had spread to her lymph nodes. As her husband received that information, I saw the resignation in his eyes that this would be the beginning of the end for him. While they had been on the outs even before she got sick, he had started wandering and had already in fact hooked up with a much younger reporter. He remained with Lisa until she felt a bit better and then asked her for a divorce. As per her usual, she went to great lengths to let everyone know that her husband was leaving a dying woman. We eventually moved her out of the residence in Brentwood, and into her estate in Malibu.

When she came back to Los Angeles from the hospital in Baltimore, she first asked me to give up all of my clients and take care only of her. At the time I was the most successful trainer and massage therapist in Los Angeles, yet I said yes and gave it all up to become her caretaker. It seemed like a no-brainer to me at the time as I had been a caretaker for so many of my brothers that had passed. I knew what to ask and how to navigate through the system. I also knew that her children were not capable, nor did they want the responsibility of taking care of their mother. I also knew somewhere inside that this would be my way to have closure. Yet to be truthful, I also had an inner neediness, a lack, an insecurity, an incompleteness. Nurturing her was supposed to help me avoid abandonment, criticism, and judgment. But that wasn't the case at all. I had no idea what I was about to get myself into. I always felt needed for my actions but never loved for who I really was which ultimately made my self-esteem plummet.

After several weeks of unwavering loyalty and dedication to her every moment's need, I realized I couldn't exist without an income of some sort. I had been making an excellent living at $120,000 a year, and since I had given up my career, I asked Lisa if she could pay me for my time in caring for her. Our practice then became one of my bringing in an invoice, and she would give me what she thought I deserved. This usually amounted to $2,000 a month, which also included any supplies that were needed at the time. I took what was given, trying my best to stay focused and get ready for the next day.

On rare occasions, I took short reprieves to cry and try to release the enormous stress building up within me. I had only Dr. William to talk to about my anxiety, and no friends to share my deep troubles with. These issues were mine, and I was deep in it with seemingly no way out as I felt I could hardly abandon her. Despite her money, fame, and family, Lisa had no one. Eventually, I started choking on my own phlegm and took to standing in the shower for thirty minutes at a time just to get my lungs to open up. Yet I never showed any sign of weakness to Lisa. I remained happy and strong for her at every moment.

Because of her quick advancement to the top of the surgical list at Johns Hopkins, Lisa lived an unprecedented four and a half years longer as opposed to the usual six months to a year given to such cases. All but one of her years was spent living a somewhat substandard quality of life. The rest of the time she spent exploring new protocols and managing $10,000-a-week cash morphine pops which very soon turned into an addiction. My responsibility began with running all of Lisa's errands and picking up her medications. I drove her to get chemotherapy every day, where I would sit with her during the treatment, and then bring her home after stopping several times to allow her to vomit by the side of the road. Once we'd arrived at the house, I would get her to smoke pot to help with the pain and increase her appetite. I would do my best to get her to eat, and then put her to bed.

We spent a lot of time together over the next four and half years that Lisa battled the disease, as I was right by her side. I stayed with her most of the time at her beach house or her place in Bel Air, massaging her aching body for hours at a time. I was with her at every doctor's visit and every treatment. But despite the best treatment that money could buy, I watched Lisa decline a little bit every day. The highlight of Lisa's end days was looking forward to when her family and grandkids would come to visit. She would spend hours putting on makeup to look anything but sick. Her efforts were quickly squandered as there would inevitably be a phone call saying something had come up; the visit would be canceled as the family member said they would instead see her next week. Lisa's heartbreak over these continuous cancellations was so painful to watch.

CHAPTER 25

Although I'd committed myself to care for Lisa until the bitter end, I had no idea what I'd signed up for. When Lisa said she wanted to go to Sun Valley, she chartered a plane for just the two of us. Once we were in the air, she sprung upon me her plan to go cold turkey from all of the medications she had been taking. In fact, she let me know, she hadn't brought any of the medicine with her. I didn't yet understand what that meant, but I soon found out. As Lisa went into severe withdrawal, her personality completely changed. Lisa had spent the last two and a half years taking a daily dosage of Wellbutrin, Celexa, and Oxycodone, as well as morphine pops every thirty minutes. The bottles had all been left on her vanity in Malibu while we flew to Sun Valley. I was not equipped nor licensed to deal with Lisa's foolish plan. And no one could have prepared me for the Dr. Jekyll and Mr. Hyde experience that awaited me.

Immediately upon our arrival, she began to demonstrate symptoms of drug withdrawal, manifesting in irritability, impatience, and raging demands. Once we arrived at her estate, we went into total lockdown. Knowing the house had been fully stocked and prepared before her arrival, she demanded that all the doors and windows were locked and that no one was to leave or enter the home. As she insisted I carry her to the jacuzzi and then back to bed every ten minutes, I slept on the floor next to her only to stay awake in fear of what might happen next. I did not get sufficient sleep for five full days. It was utter and complete hell. I wanted to call for help, but Lisa screamed at me and shut me down if I mentioned wanting to do so. I was so beat down emotionally and physically at that point, I couldn't find the strength to retaliate.

Luckily for me, Lisa's friend came over unannounced and was able to help me. Upon her arrival, Lisa became infuriated that I had disobeyed her. She threw priceless vases at me, and anything else she could get her hands on while screaming and calling me every obscene name her frail body could embrace. The trauma that it caused me was so damaging I shut down and was in complete survival mode. I was crying, shaking, and desperate to get out of the prison estate and return to LA. Eventually, with the help of an outside medical team, we were able to get her back on her medications and stabilize her condition. Once she was stable, I flew back to Los Angeles for some much-needed rest. Two short days later we were able to get her back home where she began to see an oncologist on a weekly basis.

It didn't take me long to notice the spark between Lisa and her new doctor. During the divorce, everything was on the down low. She owned a condo in Westwood and would ask me to decorate it with flowers and candles. We would pretend to go out to dinner, yet I would take her to the condo where she would meet up with the doctor. I would then return, pick her up, and take her home only to go to the condo the next day and set it up for the next rendezvous. With the divorce pending, and despite her advancing illness, Lisa was somehow able to nurture a new relationship with her doctor. I genuinely think she loved him as well as the idea of becoming a doctor's wife. I also think on some level she wanted him to save her life. This relationship was a secret, and I was the only one who knew about him.

It was during a Fourth of July party at the beach that Lisa reached over and kissed the doctor. One of her kids saw it happen and flipped out, which started a chain reaction of the kids versus the doctor. They were afraid he was going to take their inheritance as he moved in with Lisa and she promised to pay him handsomely if he married her. They traveled everywhere together, seeing every remaining sight Lisa had not yet experienced. He took her to apple and cherry festivals, to Maine and Vermont to watch the leaves change. They stayed in incredible bed and breakfast cottages and explored small towns across the nation. This was ideal for me, as it gave me somewhat of a much-needed reprieve. Sadly, the romance was very short-lived, only lasting during the first year of her treatment as Lisa's kids threatened the doctor with a malpractice suit. He and Lisa soon parted ways.

At that point, her kids decided to take over her finances. The break up was very hard on Lisa, but she was still able and quite willing to continue to see many more suitors at the condo. The kids were more or less MIA when it came to their mother. They called and asked me to make up stories as to why they couldn't come to see her. It was quite sad, as she would spend hours getting ready, so she looked perfect when they did come over. They only visited when they needed something signed or wanted something from her. They all lived within five miles of her, and could have visited anytime yet during her entire illness, Lisa was lucky to see her kids and grandkids once every two to three weeks.

Lisa's health began to fail. She was desperate in trying as many new protocols as possible, only for the side effects to be unbearable or for them to have no effect at all. Having exhausted the western medical avenues, she decided to visit as many healers as possible. So we began treks so she could experience the work and healing of Vianna (Theta Healing) and Deepak Chopra. We flew to meet as many of them as we could, and I found every single one of them to be amazing. Then she found out that a particular healer — John of God — was coming to New York and she wanted to go. I knew by then that her time was quite limited, and so I suggested that she take her daughter instead of me. She reached out to her daughter, only to be told no. Being the clever lady that she was, she suggested that she would take "the doctor" instead, knowing full well that would convince the daughter to go. I was in charge of packing for that trip, wrapping most of the garments in parchment paper. As I packed her most precious things, I knew it would be her last trip. As she got in the car to leave, she looked at me as if she too knew that it would be the last time for us. There were no tears — just a simple goodbye.

By the time she arrived in upstate New York, Lisa's lungs had filled with fluid. She did get to see John of God who came down from his chair to greet her. But it was too late. She was informed by her doctor that she couldn't fly back to LA in her condition, so she called her two sons to join her and her daughter. All three of her kids drove her back in a rented RV. She knew that that would be the only time she would have all three of her kids together and that her life was coming to an end. It was important to her that her children be part of her death, even if they hadn't been that involved in her life.

Knowing she could control the outcome of the end, when she was in Ohio Lisa called her doctor and asked what she needed to do to die. He told her to stop taking her medication. She did, and went into a coma in St. Louis. Unfortunately, after several attempts by the private nurse on hand to get the kids to pull over, stop driving and come to the back of the RV to be with her, Lisa died by herself in the back of the RV.

Yet the kids were true heroes upon their arrival back to Los Angeles, just as Lisa had wanted. As for me, she generously left me a trust. After several years of fighting, I learned that Lisa's kids had manipulated the trust twice. They had their incompetent mother sign the updated versions while she was on morphine and in the last months of her life. Finally, thanks to a great lawyer, I was able to sever my ties with the family by having a letter of absolution drawn up stating all of the actions the kids acting as executives of the will did illegally while handling my trust. In return for my signature to legally release them, my trust went to an independent firm that the family could no longer have any contact with.

It has now been almost ten years since Lisa died. It's taken me quite some time to get my life back. I spent time deciding what I really want to do next, taking stock of how I want to make a difference in other people's lives. I learned a tremendous amount about myself through my crazy journey with Lisa. With the help of my therapists, I addressed my ability to give and receive within reason, to set boundaries, and to communicate my feelings and wants. I now know how to walk away from situations that are not for my highest good, mostly to let go of the fear and understand that I am worthy of love just the way I am. Throughout this process, I've learned to love myself, take care of myself, and be responsible for myself. There is no better feeling for me in life than to love and care for others, not because I need to or have to, but because I want to. With all of this cleansing and inspired growth, I can finally say, "Thank You, Lisa."

CHAPTER 26

For much of my life, I did not have an ideal amount of self-esteem. After all, there were the many subtle messages I received as a kid that continually reinforced that thought process that it took no small amount of time or effort to quell. Being a foster child reminded me every day that I wasn't good enough. Little things such as not having the same last name as my foster parents, being a little guy with a very high voice, having to "buy" lunch with a yellow ticket — all seemed to be indicators that I wasn't going to amount to anything when I got older.

When I was a child, I wasn't initially aware of the many benefits of exercise. I was focused only on remaining in the same foster home without being moved for as long as I could. It was exercise that I turned to in helping myself deal with the difficult times and complicated emotions of being a foster child. I only knew that exercise made me feel happy and healthy. Whenever I was down, sad, or mad, and dealing with the anguish of the many emotions I experienced in my younger years, it was exercise that lifted me up and took me to my own special place. As I got older, I realized that not only did exercise help me to feel good, it also helped me look good.

I am and will always be my biggest critic. For example, I used to live in a space where I would never let anyone see my body. I wore baggy clothes except for when I taught aerobics. Then I would wear Spandex. Although I would be told that I had a great body, I felt no connection to it. I knew it could get me the attention that I craved, but that attention was usually brief moments involved in the most humiliating experiences. I didn't mind, however, because the attention was like a drug for me. Since I was all too familiar with being put down, those experiences seemed to reinforce the feelings I had for myself.

I would find myself in bars looking for someone to give me attention. I would ride around on my bike to places I knew that were hot for cruising. I took regular lovers who treated me poorly, and each time I reengaged it only reinforced my belief that many of my thoughts, feelings, and behaviors were sinful. I didn't yet realize that the people I brought around me were an accurate reflection of how little I thought of myself. Since I grew up in the Pentecostal church while living with Frank and Martha, throughout my life, I was always praying for forgiveness. It was the mantra that followed every confusing act I engaged in to find love and attention.

In my early teens, I discovered that I could compartmentalize all that I felt and all that I was. I could be the perfect boy in the eyes of anyone. While fantasizing about sex with boys and recognizing my burgeoning homosexuality, I could still go to church and sing in the choir and be an athlete at school and work as a janitor every day after school and then walk the five miles home every day. I could separate all of these different areas in my life, and I became better at it the more I did it. That pattern worked exceptionally well all the way into well into my twenties — until one day it didn't work anymore.

When all of my friends, as well as hundreds of more men around me, were dying, I knew I needed help. Therapy helped me face everything in my life that I was ashamed of and fearful of people discovering about me. I didn't realize what a heavy burden I'd been carrying. It was exhausting. I was paralyzed with fear of what people would think and say about me. Shame, anxiety, and keeping secrets were the three constants in my life. It took losing many people who died of AIDS, including many dear friends, for me to seek the help I needed to make changes. With therapy, I was able to see me and everything around me more transparent. I realized that my actions always came with reactions. I alone was responsible for the outcome.

I started little by little to stop putting myself down and change my behaviors. I observed how just that one act alone changed everyone around me. My constants didn't leave me right away, but they did diminish as time went on. Dating while being HIV positive was a big fear of mine that was continually reinforced by guys who made me feel dirty or different, a feeling I was all too familiar with. For many years of my life, I hid in the straight world, working with the very wealthy and making myself so busy I wouldn't have to deal with the anxiety related to the pressures of being gay.

But before I more or less completed my journey to health, I sought out places where I could find healing energy. For example, Provincetown, Massachusetts was my happy place. Provincetown is a small fishing village on the very end of the cape. One street goes through the town. Drag queens, crossdressers, and everything in between arrive from around the world to visit this special place, and every week a different group of people arrives to celebrate who they are with other like-minded travelers. There were the bears (very hairy), young lesbians, hardcore partiers, family week, and of course my very favorite: the Tall Ships who arrive for the Fantasia Fair.

With a history of over forty years, Fantasia Fair is an annual week-long event, conceived as a place "for crossdressers and transsexuals to learn about themselves in an open, socially tolerant environment." Over the years it has grown from mostly heterosexual crossdressers and male-to-female transsexuals, to include an entire spectrum. I would enjoy seeing the transition of a group of CEOs arrive with their wives from all over the country. Once checked in, the men would change into women's clothing and spend the rest of the week that way. It was great fun to see these men express themselves with the blessing of their wives. I have met guys and girls who have become lifelong friends and always welcome me to P-Town with open arms when I arrive. The air, the light, the people, and the energy is what always drew me back. I would visit every year and stay as long as I could because I felt safe there.

Twenty-five years later, I can look back at the man I was, and see that the only person judging me was me. As I age, I get all the usual new sets of challenges that come along with being blessed to be here as long as I have. However, I feel I'm in a much better place now to handle the inevitable challenges that come my way. I struggle with the issues that are out of my control. We inherit things from our parents and grandparents that affect us, whether it be blood pressure, cholesterol, visceral fat, or others. It's ironic that while my family didn't raise me, I still wrestle with the genetics they passed along to me. I have had to learn to accept and embrace the changes in my body. I'm challenged by the possibilities that for me it could be the HIV medicine, the HIV disease itself, and simple genetics that cause the changes such as unexplained weight gain, unwanted hair growing in crazy places, joint and muscle discomfort, thyroid challenges, blood pressure, eyesight and hearing changes, as well as mobility. I'm really good at maintenance when it comes to health and fitness. I probably notice changes faster because I remain so in tune with my movement and strength.

Yet I don't forget for one minute that it's a blessing that I'm still here. I remain one of the longest survivors of the HIV disease. I have documentation from UCLA that goes back as far as 1984 which is when they were first able to identify the virus. It's hard to believe it's been that long and I'm still here, as healthy and fit as ever. I'm so grateful that I have exercise in my life. Even though I have modified what I do, and how much I do in a day, my day still starts at 4 a.m. I run 3–5 miles, then work out with weights for an hour and a half, and either do yoga or swimming on alternate days as well. Like most anyone else over the age of fifty, what has changed the most for me is the intensity of what I do. As I get older, I find my body doesn't recover as fast as it did when I was younger. I now stretch more than I used to and take every precaution to avoid injury. It keeps me balanced and very happy.

CHAPTER 27

Along my journey, not only was I able to make essential changes, but I learned to love and appreciate critical aspects of myself that make me who I am. For example, once I'd sifted through all the muck in my life, I recognized that there are three things that I was blessed with as a child — the desire to give back, the ability to be a caregiver, and the gift to see, give, and appreciate love. I just love to give to others. I volunteer regularly, and yet I can never do enough. I have this crazy ability to see what people need before they do, and so I've always been one step ahead in providing clothing or food or just a shoulder to cry or laugh upon. I've had the opportunity to work at many shelters, kitchens, missions, and for many charitable causes all over the country. Giving back freely for me is one of the greatest gifts — and one that I will always nurture and cherish.

My next blessing is the ability to be a caregiver for others. I always have, as far back as I can remember, taken care of someone or something. It took me quite some time to know the difference between caretaker and caregiver. For the longest time, I was a caretaker: someone who gives to replace the emptiness, abandonment or loneliness that I experienced as a kid. I know I can now honestly say that I am a complete caregiver: someone who gives freely from the heart with no hidden agenda. It comes so easily to me, and I do it with the sole purpose of making sure the person's needs are met.

As a child, I made sure every kid in our family had clothes to wear, food to eat, a place to sleep, and the knowledge that they were loved. I took care of each parental figure in my life the same way and did my best to make sure they passed on with great dignity. I was there when many of my friends were dying way too young. I also knew how to work with the very wealthy in anticipating their needs and not expecting anything in return. The only aspect that I needed to learn as I grew older was how to take care of myself in the same way. It took me a long time to learn that lesson. I would give until it would either make me physically sick or until I was totally exhausted. I eventually got better taking care of me. I learned to set boundaries. I learned to say no. Those two milestones were so connected to my fear of being rejected. It was indeed a trial and error time in my life. I still struggle sometimes around saying no, and understanding and appreciating my worth. It will be a lifelong process for me, but I now have the skills to be a success.

My third and most cherished blessing is my ability to give love. One of the things I wanted most was to be loved. I wanted to be liked, even while knowing I was different. I knew even then how to brighten someone's day with a flower or a small handmade gift. I dreamed of the best stories for my friends and acquaintances and did what I could to give them the best happy endings ever as I love anything romantic and especially happy endings. I appreciate kindness and generosity and try to make that a daily part of my life. I see things about people and know that my ability to give a kind word or gesture can change their entire day. In my mind, I created this very happy place where I guess you could say the glass was always full. Exercise helped me maintain that positive feeling. Holidays are my favorite times to give presents, but aside from the holidays I will write five favorite people each month and send or give them something special. Everyone is usually surprised, and most of all appreciative, of my unexpected and kind gesture.

In the earlier days of walking my path, I used to mistake attention for love and, being a giver, would never expect anything in return. There were times during college and when I moved to Los Angeles when I thought I was in love, and truly believed I was loved, only to later discover that the romance wasn't reciprocal. When I met someone I liked, within a few weeks, I would buy them a gas grill. I'm not sure why. It just seemed to me that a gas grill was a great present and maybe they would love me more. I went to the same store to buy the grills, and so when I arrived, I would share my excitement over how this particular guy was going to be the one. Depending on my description, the owner would sometimes give me a discount, assuming that this was going to be a short relationship. I went through quite a few grills and lots of therapy before I realized that this was not an avenue of success.

I hoped I would recognize love when it came to me but wasn't sure I would. I can genuinely say I have loved a lot of people in my life in many different forms. I've always felt inside that when the person I am supposed to be with comes into my life I would know it instantly. And I wasn't wrong. Two weeks after my last Match.com date, I was volunteering for a charity, doing flowers for the tables when I looked up, and there he was.

It's amazing how the universe gives you exactly what you want even if you don't know it yourself. All I know is that I have never been happier or more content. Ray shows me and reminds every day how special I am. He lifts me up, makes me laugh, holds me accountable, makes me think, feel, and encourages me to be present and experience everything around me. For someone who has always wanted to be loved, I had no idea how fantastic being in love really is. When Ray asked me to commit (with rings and eventual cohabitation), I said yes! I still from time to time look at his finger with a ring on it and realize it's me who Ray wants to be with.

Ray is my happy ending, every day.

CHAPTER 28

Being a foster child gave me a unique perspective into the lives of children in need. I believe I know what having a family truly means. I always wished my own life was different than it was. For example, I dreamed of being in a family that shared the same last name. I wanted to be part of a family that vacationed together, and lived in a lovely neighborhood with lots of kids to play with — a family very different from the one I knew. Looking back now, I loved my upbringing and wouldn't change a thing. I now see that everything I went through — every struggle, bully, shame, embarrassment, triumph, and decision I mad — got me to where, and who, I am today. I now am very proud of who I am and where I've come from.

But the journey was long, and not without its bumps and bruises. Naturally, I can recall those times in my own life when I felt vulnerable and anxious. I was so very often afraid that I might get moved to another foster home. Then one day while watching the children's show, *Captain Kangaroo*, the Captain looked into the camera and said, "Don't worry. It's all going to be alright." I felt he was speaking just to me, and while thousands of other children might have felt the same way. At that point, I knew I would be okay.

Now I want to be that voice that comforts children. I want to be that voice that helps them make healthy choices about food, exercise, and overall wellness. A voice that tells them how to take care of themselves and others, who explains how to give back, and appreciate and love themselves for who they are. I want to be that voice which lets them know they are unique in every way. I want to tell them that they too are going to be okay, and that's why I created Trainer Tim.

Trainer Tim is an animated character I developed who is my way of being there for those children who are where I used to be. I am writing a children's book based on Trainer Tim. He embodies many essential qualities including kindness, strength, compassion, honesty, patience, the ability to love, forgiveness, healthy communication, humor, motivation, empathy, and drive. I feel that identifying and expressing these qualities can help kids make healthy choices and ultimately, become stronger and better adults. That's the voice of Trainer Tim. He's that guy who's there for the children who may not have anyone else. Trainer Tim has a message that kids need to hear. He is my gift to give in my lifetime.

I feel there's a reason I'm still here after all I've been through, and I know it's to spread the message of love and acceptance. I have been rejected so many times. Believe me, there were times when I asked myself, "Why am I doing this? Why do I keep going on?" Then I would see a child who connected with me and reminded me of why I'm here. I love what I do, and know how beneficial it is on all levels. I want to reach the kids who may not feel any hope. Perhaps they can't see a way out of the situation they're temporarily in. I know there are kids all over the world who may feel the same way I did when I was growing up. I have been truly blessed in my life and have always been provided for by the universe. Now I feel it's time to reach out, and use my voice and experience to make a difference for the vulnerable.

CHAPTER 29

I am renewed with my everlasting gratitude to those people who stepped forward to give me the confidence to live my dreams. I want to share the spiritual awareness I've reached in the last few years. Everything accelerated spiritually when I met Ray. He indeed is my very own "ray of light."

I've always believed in something more significant, more powerful, more forgiving, more tolerant and most of all more loving. I've experienced the idea of religion since my earliest years. In the Pentecostal church, I quickly learned what was acceptable and what was not. The sermons I heard were designed to make the audience feel unworthy and sinful while promising an afterlife in Hell if you didn't repent every time you went to church. I didn't accept those teachings and observed many aspects were based on service for the establishment rather than to God. I was chastised several times in front of the Dean board, which was a group of elders who governed the policies and protocol of the church and in the pastor's private study for what they assumed was my sexual preference. They accused me of acts I hadn't even performed yet (but they did spike my interest to experiment if truth be told). I wasn't much affected by the constant anti-homosexual sermons I was exposed to, although I did carry a lot of fear and shame around my desires. I knew from the very beginning that I was different and unique. It took a few more years, however, to learn that there was nothing wrong with me.

Throughout my childhood and into my teens I held on to the belief that there was something better — certainly, something non-discriminating. I'm not sure how I knew this, but I relied on my gut feeling most of the time. The little voice in my head never steered me wrong, it was when I went against that voice or my better judgment that I would get in trouble. I felt sure that I would experience a higher power with total acceptance of who we are and what we are meant to become despite the path we choose to get there.

During the AIDS epidemic, I turned to *A Course in Miracles* and enjoyed the weekly sessions that resonated with hope, love, and kindness. These messages were the cornerstones of healing and the ease of the many who were transitioning at that time. I never stopped believing in a better future, and always knew that I would find a place where I would be able to pray, meditate, and seek higher guidance. The place I discovered was actually in me. I had it all along and didn't even know it. Knowing that within me lies the answers to everything I need is incredibly reassuring. The challenging part for me was being in a place to hear the messaging and trust in who I was and what I wanted to be at any moment. I wanted to be loved so badly when I was younger that I didn't quite know that it was all around me in different forms throughout my life. When I started loving myself for who I am and what I know to be true, everything changed.

I spent my whole life striving to be the perfect person, and I have come to realize how fruitless such an endeavor is, let alone utterly exhausting. I'm perfectly healthy now, my numbers are undetectable, I look great, feel great, and move like a twenty-year-old. I have a fantastic partner who gives me back what I give him every day. I take great care of my health and never take it for granted. If I get a cold or the flu, I'm not concerned that I will die. I have great friends who are supportive, loving, and now don't feel the need to ask me how I feel. My blood is studied all over the world with doctors researching to find out why I'm still here and doing great and thriving. I am genuinely a course in miracles!

I am now so happy and full of gratitude. I wake up each morning feeling excited about the new things I will experience. I know some will be good and some not so good. When I find myself in difficult places, I stop and ask, "Creator, is the situation that is happening now in my best interest?" Then I ask to be shown what is best for me and ask how I can I handle myself in the best way possible. We each have the chance to create a new canvas for ourselves every single day. Although this is the end of this book, the book of my life is really just beginning. Despite having been born with an umbilical cord around my neck, I feel I am now just starting to breathe.

Made in the USA
San Bernardino, CA
20 October 2018